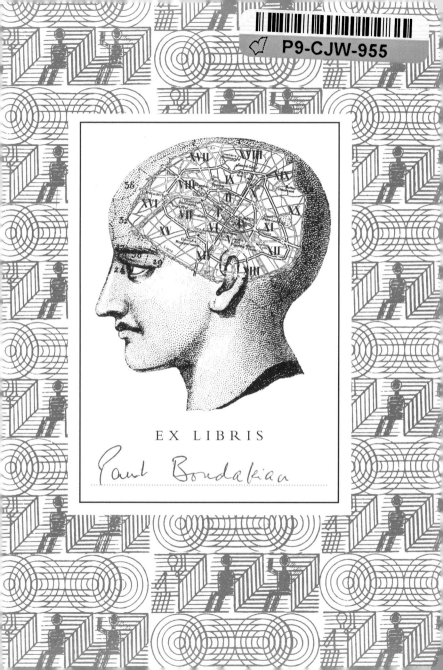

EX LIBRIS

Paul Boudakian

PARIS
out of hand

To Paul and Julia,

Beaucoup de bons voyages

Je vous embrasse,

Karen

L'Homme aux ailes voiles.

PARIS
out of hand

KAREN ELIZABETH GORDON

in collaboration with

BARBARA HODGSON
and
NICK BANTOCK

CHRONICLE BOOKS
SAN FRANCISCO

Text copyright © 1996 by Karen Elizabeth Gordon.

Compilation, photographs, and illustration copyright © 1996 by Byzantium Books Inc.

Page 160 constitutes a continuation of the copyright page.

Printed in Hong Kong.

ISBN 0-8118-0969-2

Library of Congress Cataloging-in-Publication Data available.

Book and cover design: Barbara Hodgson/ Byzantium Books Inc.
Composition: Byzantium Books Inc.
Cover illustration: Barbara Hodgson, Nick Bantock

Distributed in Canada by Raincoast Books
8680 Cambie Street, Vancouver, BC V6P 6M9

10 9 8 7 6 5 4 3 2

Chronicle Books
85 Second Street
San Francisco, CA 94105

Web Site: www.chronbooks.com

The authors wish to thank the following people for their help with this book: our editors, Annie Barrows and Karen Silver; copyeditor, Anne Hayes; Brenda Eno; Pamela Geismar; Andrea Hirsh; Marike Gauthier; Danielle Mémoire; Rastislav Mrazovac; Linda Parker-Guenzel; Grace Fretter; Camilla Collins; Guillaume Pineau des Forêts; Sylvie Bourinet; David Gay; Jean-Jacques Passera; Alain Bloch; Marisa Mascarelli; Irene Bogdanoff Romo; Richard Press.

Illustrations on the following pages have been created in part using images from the following sources:

P. 2: *L'Homme aux ailes voiles:* Used with the permission of Roger Viollet. © Boyer/Viollet.

P. 130: *O Pti Cien:* 1902: Used with the permission of the Bibliothèque Nationale de France.

Endpapers: © 1988 Edward Bawden. Used with the permission of the estate of Edward Bawden.

Pp. 55, 56, 66, 74, 142: Bowles and Carver. *Catchpenny Prints: 163 Popular Engravings from the Eighteenth Century.* New York: Dover Publications, Inc., 1970.

Pp. 41, 50, 55, 62, 108, 132, 136, 137, 145: Grafton, Carol Belanger. *3,800 Early Advertising Cuts: Deberny Type Foundry.* New York: Dover Publications, Inc., 1991.

Pp. 23: Grafton, Carol Belanger. *Treasury of Animal Illustrations From Eighteenth-Century Sources* New York: Dover Publications, Inc., 1988.

Pp. 5, 29, 113, 118: Griesbach, C. B. *Historic Ornament: A Pictorial Archive.* New York: Dover Publications, Inc. 1975.

P. 57, 141: Hart, Harold H., Hart Picture Archives. *Compendium, Vol. 1.* New York: Hart Publishing Co., Inc. 1976.

Pp. 30, 31, 35, 55, 56, 57, 107, 114, 156: Harter, Jim. *Animals.* New York: Dover Publications, Inc. 1979.

P. 142: Harter, Jim. *Food And Drink: A Pictorial Archive from Nineteenth-Century Sources.* New York: Dover Publications, Inc. 1979.

Pp. Endpaper, 64, 65, 72, 73, 82, 97, 103, 122, 136, 138, 138, 140: Heck, J. G. *The Complete Encyclopedia of Illustration.* New York: Park Lane. 1979.

P. 54: Lehner, Ernst and Johanna. *Picture Book of Devils, Demons and Witchcraft.* New York: Dover Publications, Inc. 1971.

Pp. 24–25, 59, 93: Speltz, Alexander. *The Styles of Ornament.* New York: Dover Publications, Inc. 1959.

The remaining illustrations are from private collections. All efforts have been made to credit images. Corrections received after publication will be added to subsequent editions.

CONTENTS

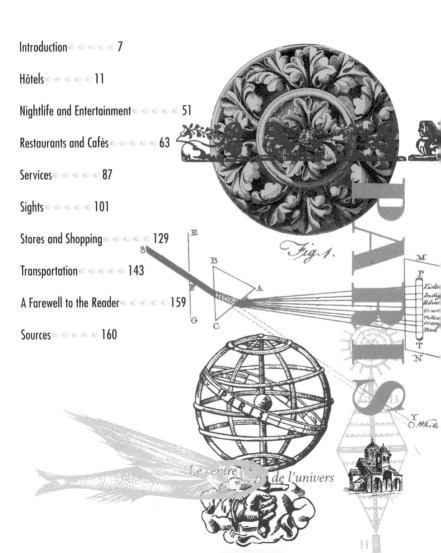

Fig. 1.

Le centre de l'univers

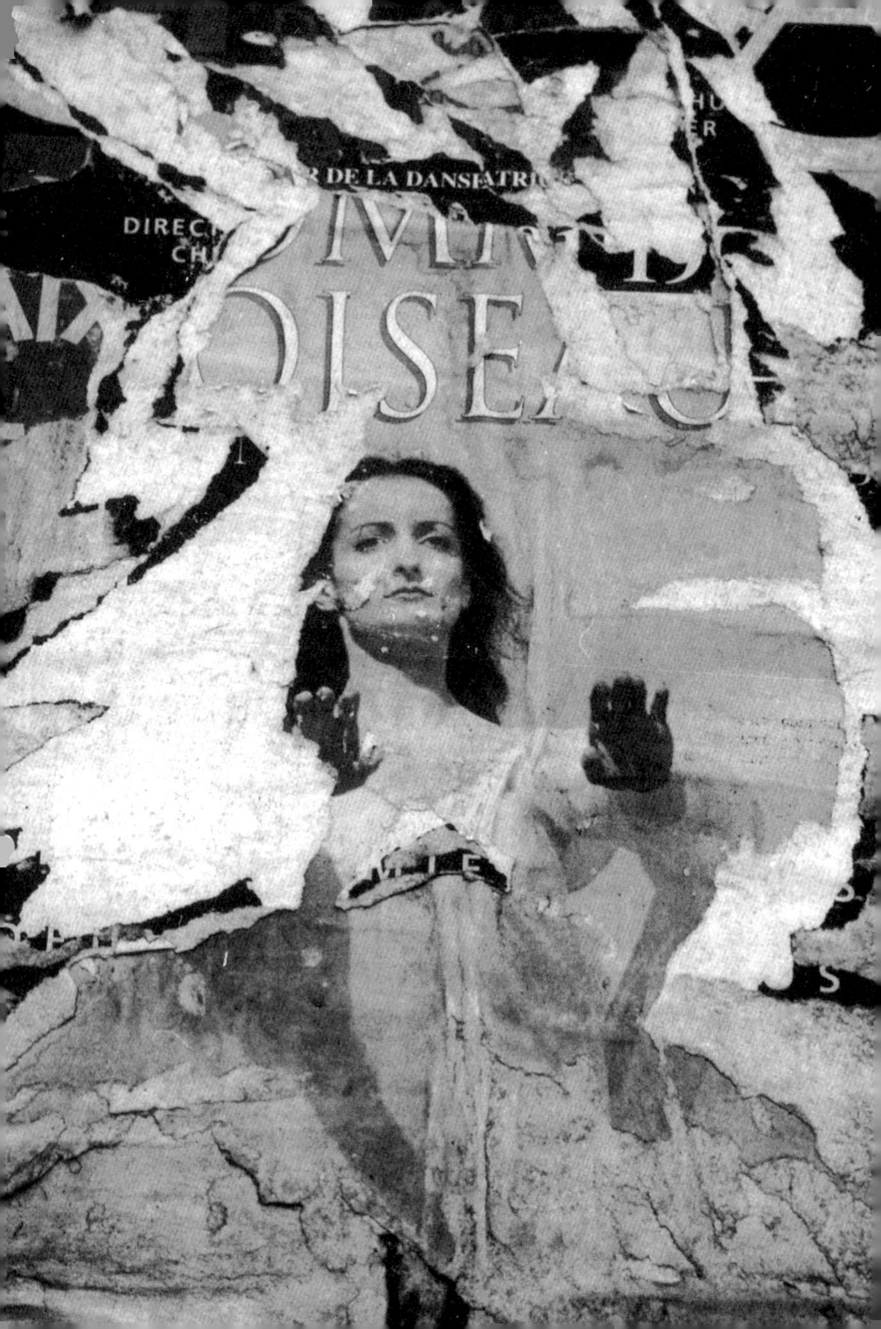
DE LA DANSEATRIC
DIREC
CH
OISE

PARIS
out of hand

Paris Out of Hand is not an ordinary guide, selling you off, before you've begun, to a Left Bank hotel or the Louvre; having handled this outlandish object, you are no longer an ordinary visitor, if you ever were. Out of hand, yet in your hand, dear reader, this is Paris by heart and Paris *par hasard,* a hopalong travelogue around the city of shadows and the city of light. Here begins a surrealist adventure through collaboration, overlapping revels of meaning, and the chance encounter upon a hotel bed of the Michelin man with a sewing machine.

Lingering over details and lunging past stereotypes and *contrescarpes,* we lead you to the brink of what might happen and abandon you to your own mischief, epiphanies, and desires. Paris, a capital city of logic, has also been the home ground for this reason gone astray, for the theater of the absurd, innovations in all the arts: how reality is perceived. Over and over, through asserting an implausible city, we reveal the one that's there, exposing its secret charms and alarms, and come up with a quintessential Paris where you will feel surprisingly, strangely at home, unpacking your own imagination in the Hôtel Aardvarkian, Triana, or Quadrille. And there's no problem getting through customs at the Apollinaéroport: it's run by the Douanier Rousseau. What's more, the rate of exchange depends more on eyes and skin, feet and laughter than on francs, dollars, and gold.

Mimicking the decorum and structure of the most traditional guide-books, *Paris Out of Hand,* through its many antic subversions, turns the pedestrian tourist into a supple and blithe explorer. Where orthodox guidebooks are told in one voice, you'll hear in this one the polyphony of today's cosmopolis, with many voices telling tales and showing the way. In fact, the city writes and paints her own book, with her tickets, money, posters, street signs—even the *Figaro* sheets of Hôtel Taupique give its guests the immediacy of Cubist paintings and poems.

Photographs, collages, maps, and graphics conspire with the text to show you what a daring traveler you've become. Hotel ratings range from benign to punishing, leaving no pillow unturned, no wallpaper unquestioned, and no sheet unlined, since beds turn into large notebooks, their occupants intoxicated with a need to record their impressions. Treating the city with honor and irreverance, taking liberties with it at every turn, this curiouser and curiouser guidebook handles the usual layers of reality with a cursory glance while introducing brave new layers and handsome forgotten ones as we go along.

Lustily iconoclastic, this guidebook gone amok licks and undresses Paris, who is herself on a journey of self-discovery, admiring her own reflection in the Seine—startled to discover *your* face looking back at her. For you matter very much in this book, and will not only find your place in it, but also make places of your own. The Paris sauntered, eaten, embraced, renewed, adored, and ever so out of hand is, for all its fabulous dimensions, details, and creatures, a city grounded in her own history, literature, and art. Through fervent exploration we found understanding and exaltation of all that Paris *is* via the Paris that *might be*.

In this runaway Paris, you may change hotels in the middle of the night, escaping the erotic excesses of Hôtel Jasmin for the cartographic drawers of Hôtel Fauteuil, the sobs and tears at Hôtel Hélas for the medieval trappings at Le Petit Hôtel du Moyen Age. If you're coming to Paris to shop, bring a favorite poem, your own for that matter, and soon you'll be sitting on it, after a visit to the pants shop Arse Poetica. And since this shop doesn't really exist, you won't have to wonder about the words bleeding in the first wash. Grand Magasin Molière, throughout the city, can handle almost any request, from drugs to insults to pork. If you want more of the latter, plus a chance to strip and wriggle in the fitting room, at Tous les Deux Brasserie et Brassière you can try on underwear while stuffing yourself with Alsatian sausage and beer.

The city will indulge your caprices, although you must accept hers as well. Don't be taken aback if you take a right turn west of Les Halles and find yourself in a sudden slice of Cairo. If you're out of Egyptian coins, a quick trip to Crédit Egyptien, with its mummy of Napoléon and hiero-glyphic automatic teller machines, will set your currency straight.

For nightlife, you can go slumming in suburbia at La Taupe Têtue, be part of the spectacle as well as a spectator at Les Arènes de Tobermory, or knock your socks off during a risqué nightclub act with the girls of La Pudeur Aux Yeux. Café Dada will break you in for the cavorting course you're on, and Café Nada will let you spy on the Paris literary scene. You may not find either café (or the streets they're on) if you consult the offi-cial *Plan de Paris par Arrondissement,* the map of Paris by district, but in reading of these made-up cafés in a fictional Paris, you'll find the real city, whose very existence and essence never cease to suggest new possibilities.

Taking yourself, finally, out of our hands, you shall place your trust in your own imagination, where all true journeys begin, with no precise itinerary, but through-the-looking-glass discoveries, for nothing is as it seems. *Paris Out of Hand* will turn you upside down, inside out, carousing and caressing you, then set you out on the streets of Paris with mind and eyes open to ghosts and shadows, enraptured passages, and multilingual laughs and whispers.

HOTELS

"In this romantic lodging-house, whose doors sometimes gape open, revealing interiors like the empty carapaces of weird shellfish, the way the premises are arranged reinforces the already dubious air given it by the rather commonplace uses to which a floating population is capable of putting it. Long corridors, like theatre wings, are strung with boxes, I mean rooms, all on the same side overlooking the passage."

—Louis Aragon

Uncomfortable beds

 Bidet in the middle of the room

 Thin walls—your neighbors can hear you

 Thin walls—you can hear your neighbors

 Double occupancy

 Somewhat more generous double occupancy

 All credit cards accepted (or excepted)

  The concierge never misses a thing

 Coiffeur attached to the hotel

 You aren't required to leave your key at the desk

 Phones in rooms. Volume assistance for those who can't speak French

 Etageliste wears a mustache (see page 33)

 Cupid stayed here

 Beds turned down, chocolates left on pillow

Beds turned down, fish left on pillow

Fire exits clearly marked

Fold-down beds

Fold-down balconies

Hotel dentist on call

Free calls home to mother

High season/Low season rates

Closed during tulip season in Holland

Cigar smokers welcome

Dreams guaranteed/Nightmares extinguished

Insomnia insured

Fezzes not required in public areas

Rapid check-in guaranteed at all times

Angora busboys

Ceci n'est pas un hôtel

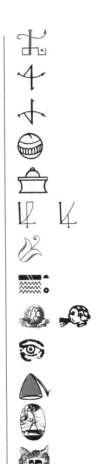

HOTEL HAUSSMANN
75, rue Dialosque

Windmills cannot be heard from any room.

The Louis XVIII bidet is no longer available.

Be prepared for long distances

HOTEL HAUSSMANN
GUEST REGISTRY

I can't believe you'd dare to have a guest register here: the duplicity everywhere in evidence is quite scandalous—in the first place not to have informed me of the name change when you replied to my request for a reservation at the Hôtel Lolo, where I'd had such a delightful stay several years ago. I suppose you think it's very funny, mocking Baron Haussmann's Boulevard mentality on a small, interior scale—but my perambulations through your absurdly wide corridors (what sort of traffic are you expecting through here, anyway—the Russian soccer team, with a merry band of *grisettes,* working-girls, in tow? or is this wide-open-spaces ambience a gesture to gauchos homesick for the pampas and their horizontal vertigo?) have shown me that some of your most picturesque rooms and alcoves with loveseats have been dismantled without a trace: number 17 with its view of number 22 in Hôtel des Apaches across the street (I remember this view well because I wound up having long confidential chats with its very visible guest—a Scottish female impersonator doing a stint at Les Monstres Sucrés), number 4 with its

Louis XVIII *bidet,* and the breakfast room so disarmingly intimate that guests just naturally shuffled in, slippered and sleeping, their dreams still caught in their hair.

The most monstrous perversity of all is that you'd ravage floor plans and the geometry of the heart in an area untouched by Haussmann's hand—innocent, idyllic, sordid, sluttish, world-apart Montmartre, whose *moulins* one can still hear creaking on windy nights, even though they're long gone. Needless to say, I am checking out and taking my sentimental attachments with me. I'll go to the Marais, if Hôtel Souci Rigoli has a room, or the Carrington, where at least you know what's expected of you, and they furnish the costumes and the props.

DO NOT CRY, TREASURED TRAVELER: THE MEMORY OF LOLO HAS NOT VANISHED, IT'S JUST BEEN VARNISHED, AT REPEATED *VERNISSAGES* (LITER-ALLY VARNISHINGS: OPENINGS OF EXHIBITIONS), IN THE FORM OF LA GALERIE LOLO.

We feel it unnecessary to describe this hotel in detail, as this rant by one guest says it all. Actually, a guest register solicited comments for a brief time, but since these were mostly vituperative, their open display drove many potential suckers away. One of our talented team distracted a night clerk long enough for another to nab the book from beneath a pile of letters (including some *petits bleus*—special delivery) that never reached their intended recipients.

HOTEL SOUCI RIGOLI
10, rue Larmonix
Guest registry

came here from the wide-open spaces, if not the pampas, of the house and studio where my friend the Argentine abstract artist El Gaucho Geometrico lives, cooks, and plays with form and light, after he insisted on winterizing my feet with a pair of Bali boots we found on rue des Pyrénées. Looking mournfully at the room, he said, "C'est une cage de lapin," and I agreed, "but a very agile one's."

The sight of the boots beneath my bed the first night so moved me that I wrote a poem on a scrap of paper and stuck half in each one. That was before discovering the *cahier,* notebook, beneath the pillow, my own name written on the inside cover beside "Hôtel Souci Rigoli." My fellow guests, the métro musicians, practice their violins, cellos, saxophones, and mattress springs when they're around, except for the two fellows from Cornwall, who spend their evenings knitting scarves and caps in *chambre* 11, the attic, if they're not turning métro cars into a riot of Celtic wailings and keenings or eating couscous on rue Pavée. The sculptor/clarinetist from Alabama has been recording my typing to blend into his composition "Concerto a Due for Clarinet and Olivetti"; it will be background music at The Village Voice for an upcoming *vernissage.*

My boots, knee-deep in the ways of the world already, put on this innocent act whenever I wish to discuss our whereabouts, geographical or metaphysical, so I've taken up smoking Gitanes—what else?—to demonstrate my infinite patience and insouciance.

—K

 Helpful vocabulary for filling out the Hôtel Souci Rigoli guest registry: *rigolo:* funny, amusing / *rigolade:* fun, a lark, amusing misbehavior / *rigoler:* to have fun, to be in harmony with this book / *juste pour rigoler:* just for fun / *souci:* care, anxiety / *sans souci:* without a care.

If your stay in Paris is to be a long one, and the Souci Rigoli is too *rigolo* for your quiet studies and indiscretions, you might consider putting up at one of the live-in hotels such as Hôtel Résidence Sainte Clementine le Charpentier. Rates tend to be slightly lower—fine if that doesn't go for the ceilings, too—and your fellow guests unpredictable in every way not covered by the rules posted on your door or discovered by the staff on hand to enforce them. In the eleventh arrondissement, with a more sedate sister in the seventh, the Sainte Clementine has rooms ranging from the small and Spartan to the wide and wonderful.

HOTEL RESIDENCE SAINTE CLEMENTINE LE CHARPENTIER
49 bis, rue des Martyrs Inutiles

 Very low ceilings

The Hôtel des Etrangers is in a building where several episodes of the thriller series *Fantômas* were filmed by Reuillade in the second decade of this century. In its present-day guise, it's more for strangers than for foreigners, although Camusian strangers won't be countenanced. Hôtel des Etrangers is open to guests and their shadows; a shadow of a doubt attracts the most attentive service. Doppelgängers are half price off-season, although they are expected to help out with the insomniacs. The hotel's policy inspired a new wine from a California vintner who stayed here in 1983: Shadow Neuf du Pape.

HOTEL DES ETRANGERS
56, rue Oncle Yquem

IN CASE ANYONE ASKS:
☛My Doppelgänger is moonlighting in another hotel tonight—he has a thing about shoes.
✳*Mon Doppelgänger travail au noir dans un autre hôtel ce soir—il est obsédé par les chaussures.*

A wish or a benediction: *faites des beaux rêves* or sweet dreams, as opposed to *un cauchemar:* a nightmare (see also page 22: sleepless nights).

Please note that for all their broadmindedness about Doppelgängers, insomniacs, and dreaming in hallways, l'Hôtel des Etrangers has a strict policy about tipping: No member of the staff will accept foreign coins from Café Dada meals. A long and violent strike, with manifestos, cleaning-woman poetry readings, shredded sheets *à la mode de* Jean Arp's torn-tossed paper, sudden middle-of-the-night room exchanges orchestrated by the striking porters (resulting in tattered dreams from which several guests never recovered or returned)—well, you get the picture: the intense emotions the Etranger's employees felt about those pastiche tips, however such coinage suits the shifting shapes of countries east and west. (Of course, once Europe is united by a single currency, all the old money will have sentimental value, and new negotiations will take place.) It is probable that the distinction between foreigners and strangers goes back to these traumatic weeks.

THE HOTEL FAUTEUIL
189, rue des Allumettes

This convenient hotel thoughtfully provides maps for its clientele. The maps, pasted into the bottoms of dresser drawers, allow guests to carry their belongings about with them while ensuring that they will never lose their way. A chain hotel, this establishment also has accommodation in Malle and Aix-les-Caisses.

⬯ A chain hotel

HOTEL JASMIN

Commentaire de nos Hôtes Aimables
Comments of Our Amiable Guests

Hey, I thought I came to this city looking for peace of mind! My friends said, "Why Paris? why not Bali or Martinique?" So what happens when I get here? The taxi from the Apollinaéroport follows rue de la Fidélité to the rue du Paradis. Fine so far; paradise where faithfulness takes you, and it's the street of the crystal merchants, as the *vitrines,* window displays, proclaim. But then we pull up right across from the passage du Désir, with thirty-two cats in heat, and a madame keeping them in *maquereaux.* Do you suppose I've had any time for the Alliance Française and the rhinoceros who teaches the *débutants* there? Like the cats between one desire and the next, I've been arching my back and rolling on it before The Burghers of Calais (who've twitched a bit in response), rubbing up against *pantalon*ed legs and Louis XV chairs, and caterwauling through the night with the rest of this *hôtel pas cher* but very *érotique.*

 maquereaux = mackerel and/or pimps

**HOTEL JASMIN
69, rue Zazie sans
Culottes**

In the *salle de bain:*
"In the pure and shining sarcophagus, sweet water reposes, warm and perfect, bride of the body's form . . . a perfume whose complex flower stirs memories, caresses or colors the indistinct desires of the naked being. . . . The mind opens its veins in a dream."
—Paul Valéry

Paul Valéry really did write this, as did others who appear later on.

HOTEL TAUPIQUE
Branches at all of the best
métro stations

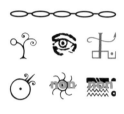

(Literature on end tables, at
the Hôtel Taupique)
"For a long time, the little
mole went to bed early.
Sometimes, no sooner had
the night darkened in her
hole than her head would
drop so quickly between her
paws that she didn't even
have the time to say: 'I'm
falling asleep.' And half an
hour later, the thought that it
was time to go to sleep
would wake her: she wanted
to lay down the earth she
believed she still held in her
paws."

—Gilbert Lascault

The city's only hotel that's actually in the métro. Two classes of room: Clochard (tramp, bum, usually with a bottle) and Luxury. The Taupique is distinguished by its linen service. In the Clochard wing, guests are invited to rest themselves within the latest edition of *Le Figaro,* and their snooze is subsidized by their more affluent neighbors. The Luxury suites' guests sleep between elegant 300-thread-count sheets printed in the latest edition of the newspaper. The sheets are changed daily so that everyone can keep up with the news. Taupique plays on not only *tropique* (the métro being *toujours* torrid), but also topical, since the newspapers the luxury suiters sleep under are always hot off the press.

On rare occasions, guests in a hurry will throw themselves into a departing métro car, clothes flapping out of *sacs* and briefcases, razor or hairdryer in hand. A face half in five o'clock shadow or a partially styled coiffure, the rest a flop or mop are a tip-off for spotting a Taupique guest.

The Taupique is a cousin to the Hôtel Taupinière, located at suburban métro stations and not entirely underground, which makes it much easier for planting, manicuring, and enjoying the taupiary gardens, too. Not all the shrubs are cut in the shape of moles: chimeras, donkeys, camels, monkeys, RER (the system that speeds through the city to the suburbs) passengers also appear. If you're lucky, while you're staying at the Taupinière, one of the gardeners will ask you to model. Then, from a nearby kiosk, you can order a set of postcards showing you in shaggy profile, or frontal view with arms and legs akimbo (if the gardener asked for a come-hither pose). If you don't mind being farther from the center of the city, this is an economical alternative, for the rooms are half the going rate of those in the more *touristique arrondissements.*

The management of the Two Taupes, as they are called for short, has a policy of hiring the near-blind to keep the hotels running smoothly: they smooth down the sheets, serve coffee and croissants to de luxers and clochards alike, greet new guests and show them to their rooms.

Obliges its guests chronometrically if not spatially. Opposite the idiosyncratic and time-will-tell Musée des Horloges et Circonstances. The only hotel that we know of where you aren't asked, "And, monsieur (madame), at what hour in the morning do you wish to be called?" Here they ask, "What time do you wish it to be?" And they can come up with any time. So the bedraggled traveler arriving at five o'clock in the afternoon can request a change of time to 9 A.M. and find himself stepping out into the fresh

HOTEL DES HORLOGES
6, rue des Horloges

PLAUSIBLE QUERY:
(Pointing to a
fellow guest, male):

↳ What time is he?
🏳 *Quelle heure est-il?*

This shouldn't be a problem at the Hôtel des Horloges:
une nuit blanche: sleepless night. Literally, "white night."

morning breeze after unpacking and washing up. Popular with former adherents of the "Jet Lag Program" who have wearied of filet mignon at dawn on Air France. A marvel of organization, the Hôtel des Horloges can accommodate travelers from every time zone.

HOTEL TRIANA
428, avenue Alexis de Taupeville

Like Au Hasard Babar children's restaurant, the Hôtel Triana is a great favorite with children —especially those on the outs with their parents, who come along *avec peur, et contre-cœur* (with fear and against their will). Most of the staff are runaways under the age of fourteen and are actually earning credit at their particular not-very-normal schools. They do tend to take the best rooms for themselves, which they never clean. The menials, however, are conscientious adults who once were lawyers, bankers, and policemen, so your own room will be immaculately maintained. If you don't mind the role reversal and can abide the occasional ruckus, this is one of the best deals in the city (true, it's not exactly well-placed for bookstores and pompous architecture), as *les gosses,* the kids, have not quite caught on to the elaborate system of deceit and expense that keeps the grown-ups' world in motion and in perpetual debt.

Hotel Quadrille

6, rue Claire

guest registry

YOUR COMMENTS ARE MOST WELCOME

NOUS SOUHAITONS VOS REMARQUES

Chambre N° 8: M. Homard. New York

I *am* fond of this hotel. It recalls my childhoods at the seaside—and it's almost convenient. I don't think I ever told you how I first came here: the travel agent who arranged my last visit to Paris was a rare one who actually spoke French (I'm glad most people in our town *don't:* the kids would be mercilessly teased) and was amused at the thought of putting a Mister Lobster in the Hotel Quadrille. He must traffic with Wonderland, too. But now a word of advice (I'm a businessman myself): You really should have a monogram on your pillows to rival the mole on the Hôtel Taupique's. But even if you were to lay my head on one such cunningly attired pillow before the end of my stay, it wouldn't soften the suffering my wife's absence caused me last night and her casual return at dawn. She is still sleeping, and smells mysteriously of the briny deep.

HOTEL TRIANA
Coomentaire de nos visitours

I am here over Easter vacation with my daughter Natasha, just the two of us, ever so nicely for a change. We've visited Le Musée Carnavalet and imagined ourselves through the centuries in Paris, as students in the medieval *Quartier Latin,* as ladies-in-waiting in the Palais de Luxembourg, as firebrands on the barricades after the Prussian siege. We had to visit Versailles to look at the gold and gaudy furniture (I kept her away from the bleeding mirrors) and Le Nôtre's gardens and fountains. I told Natasha about how Marie Antoinette used to play at shepherdess with perfumed and beribboned sheep, probably cleaner than she was: we've spoken frankly about these things. Natasha had read a children's version of the memoirs of the Duc de Saint-Simon at her Alliance Française des Enfants class in English, actually, but at least they learn how to make *millefeuille* pastry, quite an accomplishment for a child of eight. And seeing you kids running your own hotel is giving her ideas (she says she wants to be an *aubergine* when she grows up, thinking that must be the name for a female innkeeper). While at Versailles, we got off into a fantasy about the nobles playing video games there—galleries of those machines keeping the wigged and powdered old boys engaged in between their peccadilloes and enemas (at least I thought of that; as I said, my daughter's version of Saint-Simon was somewhat expunged). Then today, our last, we went to the Doll and

Marionette Museum, Le Musée des Poupées et Marionettes. Well, I just wasn't expecting some of the things we saw there—none of them were mentioned in *Paris pour les Petits,* Editions Galopin. A talking Ubu doll mouthing obscenities in every language (I recognized four of them), not only the French he spoke in Jarry's play *Ubu Roi.* More upsetting than that, however, was the collection of Marie Antoinette's dolls, in a basket, with their heads torn off, the plaque beside this outrage explaining that she played with these dolls in the last weeks of her life, to get used to the idea of losing her own head quite soon. Certainly we're used to violence, unspeakable horrors, in our own urban neighborhood, but I was rather hoping our final *sortie* in Paris would be lovely, civilized, with tea at Café Frangipane afterwards, and instead this is what we'll both remember most vividly, probably bursting out laughing as we exchange secret looks at the dinner table in Boston two weeks from now. *Merci beaucoup* for our amusing stay with you. We're leaving extra-large tips for your grown-up staff; they look a bit haggard and overworked. Have you ever been charged with adult abuse? I remember those words of Balzac: "Children! You bring them into the world, and they drive you out of it."

—Mme. Lafont

PETIT HOTEL DU MOYEN AGE
17, rue des Charmes

REMEMBER:

Une oubliette, dungeon, is related to the verb *oublier,* to forget. So take care not to be forgotten when you stay here.

Fitting head wear for *les monsieurs*

Not an oil slick, a drop of bath water

With gargoyle sink and shower fittings and dirty rainwater for washing hair, Le Petit Hôtel du Moyen Age is a place where medieval would-bes and have-beens rub shoulders, although it gets a bit clanky with the coats of mail. Here you'll also find guests speaking in stanzas from *The Romance of the Rose* and bent over *petit point* and antique *petits fours* in the velvet and brocaded lobby. A stone's throw (and remember, back then each stone repre-sented some sacred or all-too-human quality, so choose the object with care) from Notre Dame, the Cluny, St Séverin, and the clearing where logician, seducer, and holy man Abelard once addressed thou-sands of devoted students, this hotel combines primitive conditions and modern comforts with a logic you will never divine. If you want to stay in the very popular *oubliette,* or dungeon, it's wise to book well in advance, and to pack on a bit of extra flesh.

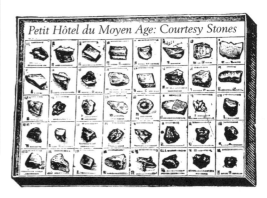

Petit Hôtel du Moyen Age: Courtesy Stones

Because of this double meaning,[84] Grand Hôtel des Echecs attracts a mixed crowd—master chess players and *amateurs* (lovers: of chess, that is), and visitors whimpering or gloating over their latest mistakes or planning their next decade of debacles. Hence the Anguish spoken is not often called for, although the language offering attracts a sad assortment of losers and sufferers seeking employment on the staff. For some, this is the next stage of recovery after a stay as a *guest* at Hôtel Hélas.

The décor was chosen to draw the first set, so you will find horsemen in the *ascenseurs* or on the twisting staircases, queens in the closet, squares everywhere you look.

Pawns scrub the porcelain and make the beds. Whatever you do, don't try to crack any jokes about "the afternoon of a pawn," or you might find yourself checkmated with death—or at least forever a part of the *other* set of guests, with their regrets, complicities, and *faux pas*.

Formerly on the grounds of the Tuileries (gardens today, once the place where tiles were made by the king's artisans), but now slightly upriver to obscure its dubious past. Each room is done in a different glaze, with matching lacquer *armoires*, closets, and trunks to stash your stuff.

GRAND HOTEL DES ECHECS
4, impasse de Godot

[84] *Echecs* is the name for chess and also means failure.

"Ici on parle angoisse"
"Anguish spoken here"

HOTEL CERAMIQUE /
CERAMIC HOTEL
22, rue des Espions

 "My wallpaper and I are fighting a duel to the death. One or the other of us has to go."

—Oscar Wilde

The following symbol means that the Forney Library really does exist. More places exist further on in the book.

 Forney Library

"In the depths of the parasol
    I see the marvelous
    prostitutes
On the side near the street
    lamps their gowns are
    the color of polished
    wood
They are walking a great
    piece of wallpaper."

—André Breton

One room, *la chambre aubergine,* is unfinished, off limits. Since *auberge* is inn, and *aubergine* is eggplant, the proprietor vows he'll change the name to L'Auberge Céramique when the triumph is complete. The Danish ceramicist is still at work perfecting a glaze that mimics an eggplant skin. But meanwhile you know how to order this much in a Middle Eastern, Greek, Serbian, or Niçoise restaurant, or recognize it on the menu, at least.

Guests frequently include *artisans,* craftspeople, who appreciate the ambience and the quasi-proximity (lovely walk most of the way, along the Seine, across several bridges and either island) to the Forney Library, where you'll find that various materials, mostly paper and its nearest relatives, and their history have been lovingly preserved and catalogued—even labels from the tackiest fast-food joints along with luscious eighteenth-century wallpapers. It was the Réveillon wallpaper workers with a grievance that set off the French Revolution, in the Faubourg Saint-Antoine. Appropriately, *réveiller* means wake up, and the people did straight away, the royalty, too late.

This has been a digression, but not unlike conversations in the butter-glazed breakfast room (like the top of a brioche, golden brown, with cream trim and details) of the Hôtel Céramique.

Petit Hôtel du Moyen Age
Guest Registry

Cher Madame and Monseigneur:

Your many kindnesses have touched me to the quick: the sandalwood soap, the ermine slippers, the unicorn hoofbeats on the roof. I chose this hotel because I was besotted with troubadour poetry when I was young enough to know better, wrote my senior thesis on imagery, allusion, and double entendres in the correspondence of Héloïse and Abelard, read *Pope Joan* while expecting my first child. I've never quite gotten over the Middle Ages (my husband still objects when I insist that he wear my garter on his sleeve as he departs for the office in our silver dragon of a Subaru), and I am enjoying the indulgences (not to mention the papal bulls) you offer this predilection of mine. The matins sung in the hallways each morning so revive my body and soul that I can skip your much too authentic *petit déjeuner*—my only criticism besides the dust, the mud, the vermin, and the warnings about the Black Death posted in the *salle de bain*. Naturally, I linger there longer than I ought, conversing with the gargoyles qua shower fixtures and the ones gargling cold water in the sink. I also like your proximity to the Cluny (the concerts gratify my sense of hearing, to which the *Lady with the Unicorn* tapestry attuned me), Abelard's restaurant, and the vein of God that runs up the haunches of Montagne Sainte Geneviève: the cloister, the churches St Séverin and St-Etienne-du-Mont, and the jewel and surprise: a Syrian Catholic church on rue Valette beneath the Panthéon. By the way, the minute I'd checked into my room, I was off to the Cluny, where a greyhound on one of the unicorn tapestries caught my eye, especially the comely curve of his tail. Later that afternoon, I could swear the same dog was curled up at the feet of a métro passenger headed toward Porte de Clignancourt.

—Sigismund Lolotte Flint-Page

Dear Madame and Monsieur,

Your hospitality has been unfathomable, by which I mean to say you have left me profoundly touched. I've appreciated the morning papers (how cosmopolitan you are—even the latest in English and Czech from Prague!), the afternoon *apéritifs*, the handsome dandies you've hired as maids. My husband and I have had time to relinquish our grudges, forget the children, go dancing on a barge by the Pont des Mercredis. He was determined to get some sand between his toes, for old times' sake, but let me stay on deck in my flats. Can a barge be said to have a deck, when it's nothing but? Forgive me, I am indulging in idle *causerie,* chatter, before my true confession. Late last night I disappeared and no doubt frightened the desk clerk when I returned at daybreak with a large salmon over my shoulder, grinning ear to ear (me, not the salmon—I'd been in delightful company all those hours). Several nights ago, at Le Chat Qui Pêche, I'd barged my way into the kitchen to sniff out a few secrets, when what should happen but the sous-chef himself asks me to accompany him to Rungis for Friday's *bouillabaisse*—that is, to the enormous fish market outside your city where all the fishmongers and restaurateurs buy their shiny wet stuff. He picked me up on the corner in his Peugeot *camionette,* and we arrived in the bustling suburbs of nocturnal commerce around two o'clock. I noticed in one café near the *grande poissonnerie* that everyone was eating ham or roast beef sandwiches with their beer, not an oyster or shrimp in sight. Fortified with mustard that could kick a horse, Jules led me through this salty wonderland, glistening with millions of flat, scaly, bloated, carapaced, open-mouthed creatures, dead and alive, in stacks, in crates, in tanks, the air a sea-soaked smoke from several thousand men with cigarettes in rubber boots, buying or selling, all strictly business except for the incongruity I was introducing as a stranger to their world. What an intense density of life—and to think that all this was but two days' catch. Every sea in the world was there, many rivers and nationalities—it took my breath away! Fortunately, I'd recently learned to breathe through my gills, so I survived that brief gasp of disbelief.

I do apologize for the shoes I left in the hallway—I'm afraid a polish and shine will be powerless against the *fruits de mer* flesh: the shellfish are especially pungent, and I stumbled into a whole mess of mussels while my eyes were popping out of my head.

—Madame Homard

HOTEL CRILLON SANS ASCENSEUR / WITHOUT ELEVATOR
14, rue des Sauterelles

 Etage (floor) 8 is called most often

 Chambre 5 *is* in the elevator

GUEST REGISTRY

I was so looking forward to my return here, after my visit two years ago (I'm the guest who was hoping to step into Maigret's shoes and remain in Paris as a bilingual cop). But why have you put me in *chambre* 5? It looks like an old elevator car, and the periodic cries of the *étageliste*[22] disrupt my uneasy sleep. I don't know where to leave my shoes at night to be polished. I'm afraid they'll fall down the shaft and forget which floor I'm on or come back smeared with whatever sort of grease is used to lubricate the cables of ancient elevators. I suppose that in a hotel so called, I should feel honored to be sleeping right in its very namesake. Did you take out the original elevator just so you could steal the name, and drag it down, from the sumptuous Hôtel Crillon on rue de Rivoli—even basking in its reputation and profiting from the confusion? Surely you get many first-time guests who are fooled into expecting at least a shabby elegance and indulgent service. Oh well, I'll be back, but next time, please, with a view of the Tuileries Sans Arbres et Fleurs (the Tuileries without Trees and Flowers).

22"What," you may well be wondering, "is an *étageliste?*" Is it the person who sits behind the hotel desk and advises people on the best vertical pathway to get themselves to their rooms? Does a hotel hire as many such employees as it has floors, or *étages,* and position them on each one to tell guests what level they're on? to recite the special characteristics of that floor and the names of illustrious or infamous guests who have also slept where you are? Well, the truth is the *étageliste métier,* occupation, can involve any word or action at all that might pertain to a given *étage.* Few hotels and apartment buildings employ them, but it's a fine career for hyperactive children, adolescents, and spry old men, and they're often deposited in a building by their mothers or wives eager to get them out of their hair or from under their feet. The whole business started with a descendant of Quasimodo's sister—one fellow who worshiped his great-great uncle and wished to make himself useful to a building or literature. Here's how the *étageliste métier* first got off the ground: this Félix Ourselard simply spent all day running up and down stairs yelling floor numbers like a demented and defrocked *ascenseur* attendant. His successors in the profession are free to improvise with movements, gestures, and cries, and some take pride in mastering the numbers from many of the world's active tongues.

HOTEL CRILLON SANS ASCENSEUR
GUEST REGISTRY

Was it Mies van der Rohe who said "God is in the details"? Whoever it was, I find God sorely missing in all the details here. I reach
for a doorknob and the *door* comes off in my hand. The chintz curtains look like a nightmare my great aunt Foxy Belle Bloom might
have had when her sloe gin ran out, and the threadbare carpet, a
nice Spartan touch, hardly makes up for the knee-deep froufrou in
your phone booth, which you must have dragged in from a brothel
during the Prussian siege of Paris when Victor Hugo was eating
rats. And the phones work about as well as they did back then. The
only place I've been able to reach so far is the underground
passageways of the Louvre: I had a fine chat in broken Franglais with
a lost guard from the Trianon. Are you the same people who tricked
out that bogus chapel on the rue du Cherche-Minuit with its relics:
Saint Barnabé's baby shoes, Sainte Clothilde de la Brasserie's tortoise-
tooth comb, Saint Ghislain's shaving brush, Sainte Mousseline's
chafing dish, Little Saint Fracas's femur bone? And why do you
make me change floors each night—just to humor that crazed old
crawdad bawling out numbers on the stairs?

—Jusko Bou Trompe
funny name, I know:
I'm a Cajun from
New Orleans

A quaint hotel run by a sympathetic Armenian family proud of their lobby graced with the painting by Allan Ramsay of Jean-Jacques Rousseau in Armenian costume. The Aardvarkian's *petit déjeuner* can sometimes include a few *bestioles,* little beasts, so you might consider consulting your guidebook with your coffee and *tartine* at one of several adequate cafés on rue Soubitil or La place des Visigoths—unless you care to summon one of the *goûteurs/euses* from the Association de Gastronomie et Manger to test for beady heads and crisp little legs.

The Hôtel Aardvarkian has an arrangement with the opulent Musée Arménien on avenue Foch, so be sure to ask for your *tarif reduit,* reduced, or for a free ticket on a special day.

HOTEL AARDVARKIAN
78, rue Sigelinde la
Bavaroise

A BREAKFAST
EXCLAMATION:
☞ There's a grasshopper/
cockroach in my crois-
sant.
☞ *Il y a une sauterelle/un*
cafard dans mon croissant.

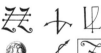

T his hotel in the Marais has an unusual history and *raison d'être* and seems to be working out much better than the conspirators dared ever dream in its beds. It all began when one architect came to stay while between apartments—waiting for the new one to be remodeled—and found the place so much to his liking that he saw no reason to leave, nor to ever go to his *atelier,* a horror near place de la République (see Services, Bureau des Bouleversements). Comrades, *copains,* colleagues—a motley gang from

HOTEL MOSTAR
15, rue des Grosses
Bêtes Ambiguës

 Special rooms
for snores

Egypt, Montenegro, Vietnam, Mexico, Lebanon, and Peru—came to visit him there, taking rooms for themselves after too much excellent wine at the restaurant next door, and they too found the hotel's hold a hard one to resist. Slowly, almost imperceptibly at first, drafting tables, blueprint paper, portfolios, and computers with amazing graphic capacities began to arrive, and not long after these came clients, announcements of competitions, designers, cheap labor from l'Ecole des Beaux-Arts. In a startling move, the original architect ended up *marrying* the hotel, after the customary zone of *concubinage*. They have not had any children yet, although he has designed a number of hotels with a bit of the original genetic (building) code and traces of his own humanity.

Rooms on the top floor are for clients only, who come from the world over and must submit details of whatever project they have in mind at the time of making a reservation. If you stay here, in one of the experimental rooms available to tourists, be sure to leave no stains on the *moquettes* (carpets) and to visit the *salle des maquettes* (models).

Don't be put off by the hyena at the registration desk: it's really a debutante in disguise. Once you have registered and received your *roman à clef,* or room key, you are presented with a flannel nightgown and some stage, diction, and gestural directions you may follow quite roughly but most assuredly during a brief appearance you are expected to make at your window whenever you please, but before going to sleep. Your audience occupies the Hôtel d'Espagne across the street (for which they pay dearly)—and then there's the usual riffraff: the foot traffic below. When a troupe of professional actors or dancers, or a random collection of exhibitionists happens to have booked into the Carrington, the prices go up even higher at the Hôtel d'Espagne, and its guests stay in through dinner, calling for room service, so as not to miss a thing. One of the most exciting shows was a defenestration performed by politicians and acrobats from Prague.

The Carrington is quite a normal hotel otherwise, except for the aquatic arrangements in several sumptuous *salles de bain* for those guests who've always or ever wondered what an amphibian life is all about. Its eccentricities refer to the life, stories, and plays of Leonora Carrington, part of Surrealist Paris once she skipped the English Channel and the debutante trappings of the upper class. The horse forests along the hallways allude to her paintings, too.

HOTEL CARRINGTON
49, rue des Enfants
Normaux

A FRANK COME-ON:
🏳️I'd like to take your hyena out for a drink. Is the staff allowed to fraternize with the guests? How about a picnic at the Jardin d'Acclimation?
🖊️*J'aimerais sortir avec votre hyène pour boire un verre. Est-ce que le personnel est autorisé à sympathiser avec les clients? Que pensez-vous d'un pique-nique au Jardin d'Acclimation?*

HOTEL HELAS
45, rue des Désarrois

Minimum three nights' stay. No reservations, no credit cards. Many languages spoken, but the blues is the Désesperanto readily understood at Hôtel Hélas.

SOME PLAINTIVE APPEALS:

☞ Don't you have larger handkerchiefs?

❋ *Avez-vous des mouchoirs plus larges?*

☞ I'd like to be alone.

❋ *Je veux être seule.*

☞ But this visitor in my bed is also broken-hearted!

❋ *Mais ce visiteur dans mon lit a aussi un cœur brisé!*

☞ Would you call us a taxi for Hôtel Jasmin?

❋ *Pourriez-vous nous appeler un taxi pour l'Hôtel Jasmin?*

Hédiard

Paris's answer to Heartbreak Hotel, although on slow nights it takes in *maladroits* and others with regrets. Solace comes in many forms, including musical, and wailing is not only tolerated but encouraged. Handkerchiefs are handed out with room keys, but this is partly to advertise the *petit déjeuner* at Café Mouchoir in *la cave* below. Budding romances among the recently bereaved and jilted are definitely not on the menu. If that's the sort of thing you're looking for, you'd be better off at Hôtel Jasmin or the Olala. Because of its euphoric/erotic properties, chocolate is strictly forbidden in the rooms.

The guest registry is the most heavily booked in Paris. In fact, many *nouvelles* and novels have begun on its pages, and the management realized *tout de suite* that they had to keep several registries going, as guests like to take them to bed, where they write their hearts out. Special pens with waterproof ink are provided, in the likely event of tears. A *scandale* arose in the '60s when Café Mouchoir was caught scraping dried tears off the china and selling them to the caterer deluxe Hédiard as a rarefied condiment for which magicoromantic claims were made. Rehydrated and bottled in lachrymals copied from those in the Louvre's Egyptian collection, the bootlegged tears went for 1,000 F per milligram and were the secret ingredient that threw the *Guide Michelin*'s restaurant ratings into disarray for several years.

Paris has never been so accessible to me, thanks to your *tiroir,* the drawer with the City of Light for its lining, my footsteps consulting the airbrushed *arrondissements* beneath my stockings and socks. I did have to hold my own against a gang of tourists from one of the Baltic countries (I could tell by the smell of salt in their hair; I have a professional nose and am here as a consultant for a special show going up at Le Musée du Parfum) who tried to wrench it away from me. When I don't leave him with his French grandmother (I'm divorced, but still on cordial terms with my *beaux-parents*), I let my ten-month-old son sleep in the drawer at the musée while I snort scents and sort them into clashes and complements. I found a baby-soft wool blanket at that five-legged sheep store, a pillow at Simrane (thinking that while his body stretches across Paris, his head will be cradled by Africa), and I must say that at the end of a day, especially on the métro, I wish I could crawl in there myself. But it's lovely to return to my room and tuck the city back into its dresser, my child into his crib, while I put myself back through the looking glass and consult a map of the heavens or oblivion till I awake with the sun in my arms.

May I comment on the behavior of your house detective? Between his insidious peering into our drawers as we come and go during the day, and his constant presence amongst the uneasy chairs of your foyer, well, it's inhospitable to say the least. It's bad enough knowing that all of Paris can get a chance to peek at our socks and scarves between the rue St Honoré and rue Richelieu, but to have that man actually pawing through our things! I am tempted to move to the Hôtel Chaussure where they personalize the bottoms of their guests' shoes with maps of Paris.

THE HOTEL FAUTEUIL

GUEST REGISTRY: PLEASE LEAVE YOUR COMMENTS **IN** THE DRAWER BEFORE YOUR DEPARTURE.

I appreciate your original map-of-Paris stationery, for the many urgent messages I've sent ahead of me throughout the city and for this farewell to you. I am here as a visiting lecturer at the Goethe Institute, at the same time examining some of the unpublished material on Rilke's life in Paris while he was Rodin's secretary—material so rarely seen that I don't trust my notes to the drawer the way some of your guests do, so jauntily slinging their belongings into theirs as they set out for the Bois de Vincennes or the Bois de Boulogne. I can't reveal the nature of this work, but I did notice a concurrence between your guests with drawers and this passage from *The Notebook of Malte Laurids Brigge,* the book that wrote Rilke's way out of what this city did to him. It almost seems that one of your more disheveled guests is running loose and torturing Malte Laurids Brigge:

> "Moist with the spittle of destiny they stick to a wall, a lamp-post, an advertisement-pillar, or they trickle slowly down a narrow alley, leaving a dark, dirty track behind them. What in the world did that old woman want with me, who had crawled out of some hole, carrying the drawer of a night-stand with a few buttons and needles rolling about in it? Why did she always walk beside me and watch me? . . . And how came that little grey woman to stand once for a whole quarter of an hour by my side before a shop-window, showing me an old, long pencil, that was thrust with infinite slowness from her villainous, clenched hands?"

I think the pencil was for Rilke, and that Rodin himself rolled the woman in an alley one night and took the map, which is why it's missing from Rilke's account.

HOTEL DES HORLOGES

Dear Hôteliers des Horloges,
My stay here has been confusing and gentle, with many outings to
awaken my mind and sort out my soul, but I am wondering what
happens to the extra hours I left on deposit with you when I
checked in with my American Express card and surrendered my
alarm clock and watch. I am certainly having an interesting time,
but is my other time acquiring interest too?

> *I was on rue du Cherche-Midi the other day long enough to see the
> signs change as the evening wore on. Yup, rue du Cherche-Minuit
> they all started saying, and I'm still looking for them both.*

View is superb! Old lady on distant balcony shuffling by every ½ hr.
—M. Duchamp, *Chambre* 12

> *Does she supply the fish for the pillows?*
> —*Teresa Carpestrato,*
> *Room 16*

Perhaps she has been hired by the neighborhood to act as a cuckoo
clock and shuffle out on the ½ hour?

> *Did you stay long enough for her to announce the passing of the*
> midi *and the* minuit?

You show-off. Why can't you just say noon and midnight?

> *You chauvinist. This is France, so let us speak frankly here.*

HOTEL RIEN PLUS
222, rue Simon
le Simple

This hotel does not accept guests. They advertise, accept reservations, send confirmations, *and* solicit advance payment (accepted by check or money order only), but no one has actually ever managed to stayed there in its entire seventy-five-year history. It's worth making a reservation there just to see the Bureau de Déception. But be warned: those who have been foolish enough to make a deposit have never been successful in getting a refund.

HOTEL DES MUGUETS
324, rue de Sainte-
Marguerite

SOME LIKELY
REQUESTS:

☜Please ask the maid to polish my doorknob; I'm expecting a very distinguished visitor.

✝*S'il vous plaît, pouvez-vous demander à la femme de chambre d'astiquer ma poignée de porte; j'attends un visiteur très distingué.*

Originally called Relais du Mois de Mai et des Muguets, this inn shortened its name in 1978 and ever since has paid the consequences with a change in the clientele attracted by the remaining syllables. *Muguets* are lilies of the valley, which the French assiduously send and deliver to one another on the first of May. The inn began with an abbreviated *ouverture annuelle,* annual opening, long before it knocked those extra words off its sign, offering its hospitality (beds, food) only during the month of May, the one time of the year when Madame Pugnol, the original proprietress, was not too grouchy to receive and tend to guests. *Muguet,* however, also means gallant, flirt, fop, and *mugueter* means to flirt, carry on, so when the name was abbreviated, the place became a haven for all sorts of loaded rabble (prices are quite steep) looking for cheap thrills after a titillating stroll on rue de la Frissonière, just around the corner.

Since it's become a venue for liaisons, Hôtel des Muguets prides itself on being the very soul of discretion. A leering wink from night shift reception can be disconcerting if you don't understand. They will gladly divert calls if you alert them to your needs. An embarrassing form to fill in (optional, *naturellement*) is offered should you require special services. But sometimes they go too far! We've heard from more than one guest that when a wake-up call was requested, it came in this most understated form: a note slid under the door.

MORE LIKELY REQUESTS:

🖝 Please don't accept any calls for me from New York tonight.

✝ *S'il vous plaît, ne prenez pas d'appel de New York pour moi ce soir.*

INSTRUCTIONS FOR YOUR HOTEL ROOM AT THE HOTEL DES MUGUETS:
Note the particularly helpful directions for
IN CASE OF FIRE!/EN CAS DE FEU!

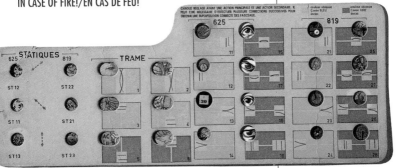

Hôtel Jasmin
Guest Comments

Back at the hotel I lie in bed not so much out of
habit as necessity: there is no place else to be. The
floor of my room is covered with feathers, for my incubi, of
seraphic appearance if not manners, are stupid enough to do
their molting in winter, and they tend to go in for rough play.
The room is otherwise also quite enchanted, which is not its
only charm. I put a glass to the wall to hear what Polish sounds like,
but the voices soon break up into laughter and the glass shatters in
my hand. Then I try putting my shoe to the wall and hear my own
footsteps disappearing down the passage des Grands Cerfs, the passage
of the Big Deer, on my itinerary tomorrow. I will visit a studio where
kites, *cerfs-volants:* flying deer, are being made from designs by artists
throughout the city for a special exhibition at Le Musée de l'Art
Moderne. I'm always a day's footprints ahead of myself, which is quite
a handful for the fellow who polishes the shoes each night.

—Yolanta

Hôtel Jasmin
Guest Comments

I know this hotel is supposed to be sexy, but I was truly
shocked, returning at 4 A.M. from an orgy at place
d'Italie, to find the shoe polisher moaning and
rolling on the floor with ten left shoes belonging
to guests whom I must face at breakfast.

—Alfonsi Lombardini

GUEST REGISTRY: HOTEL HELAS
HISTOIRES DE NOTRE CLIENTELE SOUFFRANTE

I don't consider myself a battered woman—that's certainly not what brought me here (with my own handkerchiefs, I'll have you know: yours are much too thin for the kind of tears I've been wringing into my bed)—but an innocent trip on the métro today threw this into question (I know we're supposed ~~to~~ stay in our rooms, but the bombshell from Beliz~~e~~ on the floor above me was pummeling her pillow with such ferocity that bits of ceiling plaster were flaking into my distressed hairdo, and my mournful trance was jerked loose). When I checked in at Hôtel Hélas, you did check me over and take inventory of my many *blessures,* not blessings but wounds, both physical and emotional, so you'll know the set of bruises on my left shoulder that played such a starring role between Gare d'Austerlitz and Sabot. I was in those seats you're not supposed to sit in during rush hour, the ones that make such a delightful thwack when you get up and let them go, when all of a sudden the fellow facing me clapped his hand onto his right shoulder (mirroring my left—and we were nowhere *near* Métro Miroir) and exclaimed most emphatically that only a man could have left such marks on me. When I lied, saying, "No, I'm clumsy" he insisted that bruises in that place had to be male in origin, and that I was *battue,* beaten up. And he simply had to go on with the drama, recounting roughly how it happened, after making love (some obscene gestures I'm too untalented to draw in this handsome album), and making sure everyone in the métro car was participating in his speculations and partaking of my pain. Well, I was both disconcerted and amused by his madness while enjoying the memory of the bruises' and my true history, but when we both got out at the same stop, I decided things had gone far enough, and left him with some bruises of his own. Thanks for the restful, restoring time I've had here. I'm wanted again at La Brasserie des Mauvais-Garçons Manqués, where the customers are beginning to miss my hot chocolate cookies and *tarte des galopins.*

Hôtel des Muguets

 My lover has a mother in Istria who's a Goldoni, hence a Commedia dell'Arte, aficionado, and so when I happened into a theater bookshop on rue Bonaparte, I couldn't resist buying her a copy of a magnificent book on commedia I found without even looking. The bookshop was a theater itself, on this occasion, with an older lady dropping a packet of engravings on her foot, and all the women in the shop repeating cries of sympathy, while an intense young Italian theater director begged to know where to find a certain book, and a small, composed, attractive woman named Colette watched everything with smiles flickering through her eyes and face before passing out masks and assigning us our parts for the next improvisation.

I am a Laplander, a Laponais in your very strange tongue, and I partly chose this hotel because I am not accustomed to a great deal of light, of which I see enough here when I am out sight-seeing. I visited the Bastille area today: the big shiny opera, the galleries, shops and place des Vosges, whose architecture and pink stone are so unlike anything at the Arctic Circle, and rue de Lappe, which I was sad to learn has been a street of danger and crime. Now that I think of it, one of the Maigret mysteries (yes, they are translated into all the Scandinavian/circumpolar languages) is set on rue de Lappe. I wish the guidebooks wouldn't say this to everyone who visits Paris: they might put the names together and have the wrong impression of my land and people. My stay here has been very unthreatened, except that I am not used to cars, and I believe you have more than most places do, so I must be very watchful and quick. Perhaps next time I will travel with my dogs, whom I left at home with the reindeer. I was very touched when your *patron* told me that you could accommodate them, since your blind staff have their own dogs on the premises. That way, mine could get to know canines from another culture and learn some metropolitan manners.

I am not the unreasonably grateful or astonished visitor to Paris; one further step and I'd lose all gratitude for having come this far. Still, I continue to cross the bridges that are the inalienable ritual of my implacable boots, over le Pont Louis-Phillipe, le Pont l'Archevêché. The Seine from le Pont l'Archevêché rushes beneath in a tenebrous gutter of muttering sound, something swirling beneath it that is more than water and mud, the memories of *clochards*. And if anyone in Paris loves, it is these bundles: I have never seen such a look of ardor as I once saw on a *clochard*'s face regarding his *chocolat,* which is a bottle when it's full—it's a *cadavre* when there's nothing left—held in his arms with infinite tenderness and longing, and the tenderness was returned. The river is their hotel. Voices, voices everywhere: what it means to live in a city, what it means to be anywhere.

—Tamara Chagrinsky

My legs were kicking up and my heart was jumping and I shoved myself out the door and into the métro and into the Jeu de Paume, where I noticed that the only *salle* that is *climatisée* (air-conditioned) is the Salle Gaugin, as if his paintings were radiating a tropical heat and the room needed cooling down. After I left, much later, toward the point where afternoon and evening begin rubbing against each other, I felt like walking and wandered around the streets in the very approximate direction of home, and the streets were suddenly deserted, and very still, and began to turn black, the very walls of the buildings, even before the sky opened, seemed to become wet all by themselves, like a cave. And then a deluge followed, so immediately that I didn't know what to do with myself: it was almost like being fired on, and all I could do was run. Well, I kept running and dived down the first hole I saw (rather like *Alice in Wonderland,* she thought) and still had no idea where I was. The hole turned out to be the Trou des Halles and eventually the métro I, soaked rat that I was, badly needed then. There is something so reassuring about the métro stations. Even if you have no idea where you are above ground, you can locate yourself below—many times I have felt that sense of safety and familiarity underground, as if I were in the arms of the Great Mother, the *primum mobile* of the world.

—K

HOTEL DES HORLOGES

Dear Monsieur et Madame,

You are a little less dear this morning than you were yesterday evening when I came into the *bureau* to borrow *Paris par Errondissement* and have a cup of *chocolat*. I asked you then for a wake-up call, for a very important meeting I had today at La Bibliothèque de L'Histoire de la Ville de Paris, and you were all smiles and graciousness and understanding about the urgency of my waking on time. I was counting on you, since you discourage your guests from bringing their own alarms and disturbing the clockworks here. So at 10:15 I awoke, stunned from too much sleep and heavy dreams (I do have a watch for use in the city), in quite a panic, splashing water on my face and dressing faster than I've ever undressed, and when I opened the door, what should I see at my feet but my right shoe with an alarm clock in it ticking away peacefully. So this is your idea of a wake-up call? Maybe the cow who is now the leather of my Ferragamo flats was somewhat aroused when your *réveille-matin* rang, but I didn't hear a thing. I was able to patch things up with the *directrice* at the bibliothèque. Fortunately, she knows about this place, and said had she known I was staying here, she'd have offered to wake me herself.

Small mishaps tend to bring out the warmth in people who are basically kindhearted (as she seems to be), and as I am one of those people, I am inviting you to have a drink without me tonight at Aux Déboires de Petrouchka.

—Aurora Schlaffenfuss

PALACE

éon — Tél. Fleurus 27-89

UIT

US LES JOURS

ris et Matinée
FÊTES

R PLACE

ur Réunions, Fêtes, Cours
lation, etc.
— PRIX TRÈS MODÉRÉS
US (9°) -I- Tél. Trudaine 88-89

SCRUTIN   SCRUTIN   SCRUTIN

NIGHTLIFE *and* ENTERTAINMENT

"Paris, Paris. There is something silken and elegant about that word, something carefree, something made for a dance, something brilliant and festive like champagne. Everything there is beautiful, gay, and a little drunk, and festooned with lace. A petticoat rustles at every step; there's a ringing in your ears and a flashing in your eyes at the mention of that name. I'm going to Paris. We've come to Paris."

—Nina Berberova

No. 08
Valable en catégorie J-3   jusqu'au
Valable en catégorie   jusqu'au
Valable en catégorie   jusqu'au
Nom : AUFI

L'ÎLE SAINT-LOUIS

re le dancing
le coca-cola

7952

CARTE D'IDENTITÉ

Barthélemy

VINS SPIF CE
ET

ES RETENUES

DUBONNET

367 Mᵈˢ D'Or
Membre du Jury
86 Mᵈˢ 1ʳᵉ Monte.
86 Mᵈˢ D'Arg.
1 Membre du Jury
888 Mᵈˢ D'Or
82 Mᵈˢ D'Arg.

MAISON FONDÉE EN 1846

Maisons de Vente

72 Av. Victor-Hugo   121, B.ᵈ S.ᵗ Germain
L.B.⁴ Denain   7, Rue du Havre

ÉPÔTS

Société Anonyme Capital 1.250.000

CONTRE REMBOURSEMENT

CARTE INDIVIDUELLE D'ALIMENTATION - Titre

THÉÂTRES, CAFÉS-CONCERTS, ETC.

ir la liste ci-contre où l'on trouvera les adresses
les numéros de téléphone des principaux établissements.

Métropolitain   0   MÈTRES   500

"Shepherdess O Eiffel tower whose flock of bridges bleats at the morning"—Guillaume Apollinaire

Les Folies-Bergère, Le Moulin Rouge, and Le Chat Noir were the most famous of the cabarets celebrated in art and the collective memory, Toulouse-Lautrec's posters, and songs that still billow around the evening sky of Montmartre's place du Tertre. The various *folies* started out for light opera and ballet, but these were kicked out of the way by the cancan and other entertainments of the cabaret, with luminaries like Aristide Bruant and dancer Jane Avril drawing adoring, astonished crowds from across the English Channel as well as from the Champs-Elysées and the Latin Quarter. I won't go into the origins here; Théophile Goulugue has done such an apt and rambunctious history of these funhouses in the admirably translated *Guide Rouge,*[2] that renegade, none too subtle send-up of the stalwart, strict *Guide Bleu.* Suffice it to say that *Bergère* did once refer to a real live shepherdess who went mad when she lost *all* her sheep, one by one, during her first weeks at the capital of glamour, fast living, and *artistes*—paralleling her loss of innocence, layer by layer, stranger by stranger, *impasse* by gaslit or darkened street. When her brother finally found her, astray and disheveled at a tavern in Belleville, he carried her off to their uncle's casino in Monte Carlo, where

LES FOLIES-BERGERE

32, rue Richer

[2] About that *Guide Rouge:* You think morals are loose, that anything goes these days. Hah! The truth is, my publishers have forbidden me to quote from this book, considering it too racy for the American pulse, not to mention the German, Italian, Slovenian, Danubian—imminent translations of *this* guide. <u>Théophile</u> means he loves a god, but *Mon Dieu,* his poor mother, I don't think *his* god spends much time at the altar of St-Germain-des-Prés. But here is a curious coincidence: *pré* means meadow, or field, and it was through this very urban meadow that our shepherdess was straying in the losing of some of those sheep—although some found the grass greener across Paris and headed for Montmartre, which quite finished them off.

her newfound wisdom of the ways of the world was harnessed to her congenital pragmatism and trebled the casino's takings over the next five years.

LES FOLIES-BERBERES
245, rue des Eponges

This Berber spin on the cabaret is in the colorful *quartier* of Barbès, where every western male tourist should buy himself a new outfit and throw away his pants. The Folies' original scope has expanded to include all manner of North African female talent, mostly in music and dance. The third Friday of each month is a massive improvisation, often with some of the razziest *rai* musicians making an unannounced appearance.

LE TROTTOIR DE BUENOS AIRES
37, rue des Lombards

Here you'll find a tango nightclub with classes on Saturdays. Always a great pleasure to watch the bandolino bouncing upon the red handkerchief covering the bandolinier's knee. The array of snacks available embraces all of Latin America, depending on who feels like cooking, who's not too busy with political causes on a given day. Once a year, on August 26, the whole show moves to the Pont des Arts to celebrate the birthday of Julio Cortázar, so often cited by Argentine Parisians as the author of each coincidence that makes their lives worth witnessing.

A reversal of a striptease, although to sustain the so-called *pudeur,* modesty, the girls begin wearing boxer shorts and athletic bras. To the provocative drive of drums, zembas, and piccolos, Nanette, Lily, Virginie, or whoever she is adds item after item of clothing upon her rigid form, from her toes up to her ears. Sunday evenings you might make an effort to come early and bring along some of those shirts and tennis shoes you wonder why you ever packed: it's the night when members of the audience toss garments onto the stage for the performer to tauten herself into, and it's generally the most gratifying performance of the week.

Paris would be dull indeed with only one amphitheater, the Roman Arènes de Lutèce, and all it took was one good man crazy in love with his cat to set the plans in emotion on a chosen construction site. Señor Le Brun simply wanted a cultivated setting in which to promenade his cat Tobermory—who'd have none of such nonsense but swiftly cleared the area of its notorious rats.

As for you, cherished visitor: consult your *Pariscope* to see what's on. The place has attracted a dazzling array of *artistes* and some *very* mixed-

NIGHTCLUBS
LA PUDEUR AUX YEUX
189, rue des Perditions pas Graves

A note about the name and the meanings vying for your attention: *La poudre aux yeux,* powder in the eyes, is the French version of pulling the wool over someone's eyes, or throwing dust into them if no sheep are at hand.

AMPHITHEATERS
LES ARENES DE TOBERMORY
400, rue Guillaume depuis la Rapprochement

A few things to take along to Les Arènes de Tobermory

Zepo le Brun, a half-Portuguese fisherman (sea-set eyes and rolling gait from his mother's side) who came to settle in Paris after making his fortune in lobster and related crustaceans—another coup all for the love of the first Tobermory.

One of these, known to the Buffon crowd as Le Grand Crème, had been wreaking considerable havoc among the cheese shops of the area, so in gratitude, the cheese merchants scratched up some coins to toss into the arena project as well. With its fast-growing international prestige, the cheese dealers take great pride in their neighborhood cultural center, and sponsor occasional comedy nights they call La Vache Qui Rit, after the Laughing Cow merchandise they hawk so liberally.

up crowds. Les Arènes de Tobermory have been the venue of an open-air international film festival, inspired by the one in the coliseum of Pula in former Yugo bla bla. This is no coincidence: the promenade night (see facing page) is very popular with refugees from the former Yugo bla bla who are homesick for the evening *corso,* where everyone strolls and visits outdoors. Drama festivals, performance artists, dance, and music all have a place here to do exactly as they please. It was at Les Arènes de Tobermory that the Quartetto Boccacciano played the only prank in its otherwise distinguished repertoire, *The Table Quartet, Quartetto di Tavola.* Padding out to center stage, the four musicians opened their violin, viola, and cello cases and drew out a dinner party. From the cello case came an unfolding table with silverware, glasses, plates (crystal and china, it was advertised after the final movement, was from the showcases on rue de Paradis), while from the rest emerged the *entrée,* which in France is the *first* course—although in this case it was called the *allegro,* something light to bring on an upbeat ambience. A waiter appeared with *le plat principale, andante,* on which the quartet dined in leisurely fashion while earnestly conversing; at this point the audience was doing so, too. The cheese course, a *minuetto,* was provided and served with great flourish by the neighborhood *fromagers* (somewhat minuet in motion: they had practiced beforehand with an eighteenth-century dancing master), who also distributed bite-size samples of many fine cheeses to the audience, by now growling with hunger and intolerant of any further delay in its gratification. Dessert and coffee, a sort of two-part *allegro vivace,* rounded off the evening and a most satisfying performance, as the quartet declared afterward to the press.

Under normal conditions, Thursday nights are closed to performances: it's the evening of *La Grande Promenade,* when all the audience has to see and hear is the rest of itself, and individuals see themselves reflected in the eyes of their fellow human beings. It's not the same as strolling on a boulevard or eyeing one another from a café table: here the terrace is multilayered, and the shape/direction is always some variation of the spiral. Some dress up, some dress down. Women have been known to parade in their slips as often as in weary ball gowns. Bring snacks, flowers, your pedicure kit—whatever your twilight desire—but above all bring your innermost feelings in extroverted packaging and some serious stalking shoes.

Note: There's nothing to the speculation about Zepo, Tobermory, and the street called Le Chat Qui Pêche, The Cat Who Fishes. Tobermory is afraid of water and won't even eat the lobsters and *langoustes* if their shells look too wet.

NIGHTCLUBS
LE SINGE SOULE
THE DRUNK MONKEY
88, rue de la Renonciation
45, bd Jean Genet
128, rue Maldoré

Le Singe Soûlé, like Batifol, is one of several establishments scattering themselves through the city in susceptible districts, in this case Montmartre, Montparnasse, and L'Autremont (métro Ducasse). The chain takes its name from a popular spot of La Moche Epoque that did have a monkey on its premises, until too many of the regular revelers realized what he was up to, picking their pockets, and made their feelings known to the *patron*. Nowadays Le Singe Soûlé attracts a younger, rougher crowd who know better than to have pockets and rarely arrive before 1 A.M.

NIGHTCLUBS
LA TAUPE TETUE
61, rue Shalimar

If you feel like slumming, this might be the place for you, but don't drink the house wine or *eau de vie* if you need your head for anything the next day.

For your vocabulary:
gueule de bois: Hang-over, literally "face of wood" (*see also page 65*).

Une taupe têtue, or a headstrong mole, is someone to reckon with when you consider the strength of its hands, so the club attracts quite a tough crowd. This all-nighter is in the suburb of Drancy, on the ground floor, or *rez-de-chaussée,* of the former *mairie,* city hall. The *tête-à-têtes* to be had here are not the *salon de thé* kind, and when discussion ceases, a tussle in the dirt is often the next step, which is why the floorboards were removed. The funny thing about all this is how popular La Taupe Têtue is with the same fine ladies who frequent the Ecole de Fontainebleau *toilettes,* and it's quite a treat to see them stripped of their decorum and hauteur, tearing out each other's hair and rolling on the floor.

Outdoor cinéma on the Pont Neuf with movies projected onto the Seine. Tickets include foot passage over the bridge. Clement weather only, April through October. Viewing times dependent upon sunset and smoothness of the river. Well known for continuous screenings of *Orpheus.* Bring your own chair.

The Pont Neuf cinéma became an historical edifice when one night's screening slipped away from the projector and started to flow gently down the Seine. The audience, without hesitation, leapt up and ran along the embankment so as not to miss a moment of the movie's journey downriver.

A pillow on our visible bed. The fish looks into the dream, the pillow turns into a miniature air mattress and floats down the Seine, with a doll as passenger. It just so happens the Pont Neuf cinéma is showing a midnight series, and the doll floats into one of the movies and finds what she's looking for: a stolen watch in *Les Enfants du Paradis.*

CINEMAS

THE CINEMA ON THE PONT NEUF

THE LONG HISTORY OF THE PONT NEUF AS A PLACE OF ENTERTAINMENT

"Three times in February the river rose again above danger-level. 'Even the Seine wants to see *Chantecler*,' people said; for Rostand's brilliant comedy of the farm-yard—in which Montesquiou was enraged to find himself satirised as the Peacock, *'prince of the unexpected adjective'*—was playing at the Porte Saint-Martin. . . ."

—George Painter

CINEMAS
L'ANGE DES SABLES
88, bd Pépin IV
Métro et Pont: Bir-Hakeim

"Monsieur Desroches, you and I will go to the theatre for nothing!" cried Huré to the fourth clerk, with a rap on the shoulders fit to have killed a rhinoceros.

Then followed a chorus of shouts, laughs, and exclamations, to describe which we should have to use all the onomatopœias of the language.

"Which theatre shall we choose?"

"The Opera," said the head-clerk.

"In the first place," said Godeschal, "I never said theatre at all. I can take you, if I choose, to Madame Saqui."

"Madame Saqui is not a play," said Desroches.

"What's a play?" retorted Godeschal. "Let's first establish the fact. What did I bet . . . ? tickets for a play. What's a play? a thing we go to see—"

"If that's so, you can take us to see the water running under the Pont Neuf," interrupted Simonnin.

—Honoré de Balzac

L'Ange des Sables, an absurdly vast and arid cinéma run by a fanatic from Fez, shows only movies shot in the desert: *The Sheltering Sky; Gallipoli; Le Petit Prince; The Red Desert; The Misfits; A Night in Casablanca; The Tattooed Map; Where the Green Ants Dream; Zabriskie Point* (as well as Antonioni's and Bergman's films of deserts in the soul); *Blaze On, My Little Tumbleweed,* and plenty of other westerns.

Since the atmosphere is dehydrated in this cinéma, and its visitors leave feeling quite parched and scorched, an après-desert visit to Café Frangipane or the more convenient Caravansérail d'Oubli will replenish your electrolytes. For further refreshment, there's always a dip at La Piscine Pontoise or Jean Taris, which the management of L'Ange des Sables preposterously suggests you reach by swimming up the Seine and crawling through a jungle movie in progress at Le Cinéma Pont Neuf.

SMALL TALK IN THE SAND:

≪How many angels can dance on a grain of sand?
≫*Combien d'anges peuvent danser sur un grain de sable?*

≪I am one thirsty angel.
≫*Je suis un ange vachement assoiffé.*

$\mathcal{W}$ent to Le Divan to fetch a copy of Danielle Mémoire's *Dans la Tour.* Lovely walking in the tickling rain, letting it coif me, because my hair is cut, still long, to let its curls twist around in varying shapes. There's a bit of a smack in the air. Walking back toward Belle-chasse circuitously, I happened upon La Pagode, a Chinese-architectured cinéma with a tea room all glass—walls and ceiling and a garden of branches and stones, wet and shining among fallen brown and green leaves. So I'm having a coffee at a low black rattan table. Everyone looks small because we're all sitting rather close to the floor (see Services, *Laveries*).

CINEMAS
LA PAGODE
57 bis, rue de
Babylone

LE GRAND BAL TRAVESTI-TRANSMENTAL

You might also want to flip back in time to 1923 and join the crowd at the *Grand Bal Travesti-Transmental* organized by the Union of Russian Artists, and thus described in the program announcement:

"This is going to be a vast fun fair. There will be chariots, traffic jams, competitions to choose beauty queens, gigolos and gigolettes, bearded women, pigs, merry-go-rounds, fake massacres, a four-headed foetus, mermaids and mythological dances, and oddities made of flesh and unbreakable wire, which are at the same time fire-proof, insured against accidents and safe for children of all ages. Delaunay will be there with his transatlantic troupe of pickpockets, Goncharova with her boutique of masks, Larianov with his "rayonism," Léger and his *orchestre-décor,* André Levinson and his all-star company, Marie Vassilieff and her babies, Tristan Tzara and his fat birds, Nina Peyne and her jazz band, Pascin and his original belly dancers, Codreano with her choreography, Iliazd and his bouts of fever reaching a temperature of 106, and many other attractions. The ball-rooms will be decorated by the best artists of today."

—Sonia Delaunay: Rhythms and Colors

RESTAURANTS *and* CAFES

"I haven't eaten anything for two days, Olivier," Proust declared, "I've been writing; but first I want very strong black coffee, double strength, so," he added earnestly, "you mustn't be afraid to charge me double for it on my bill." When he left his pockets were empty, and all but one of the staff had been fantastically tipped. "Would you be so kind as to lend me fifty francs?" he asked the door-man, who produced a wallet of banknotes with alacrity. "No, please keep it—it was for you. . . ."

—George Painter

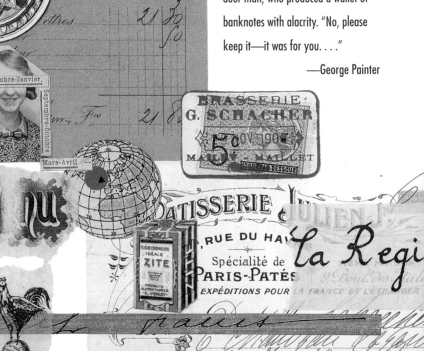

Table sharing mandatory but privacy guaranteed

 Rotisserie on premises

 Excellent *profiteroles*

 Fauning service

 Open very late

Open very early

 Excellent service

 Arms-length service

 Avoid the *plat du jour*

 Cutlery supplied

Carelessly modeled on the porcelain pavilion at Versailles, the Petit Trianon de Dégustation is, like its prototype was to begin with, a fine place for a loll and snack. It does pander to aristocratic pretensions, so wear your powdered wigs and high heels (especially you men), and don't forget your *mouches* (flies: beauty marks beside your best features). What's offered for tasting revolves at the whim of the visiting chefs, who are on holiday from *plats du jour* of their usual menus, and are amusing themselves as much as the mugs of the impromptu guests. When two of these culinary *vedettes,* stars, wind up in the kitchen at once, diners are in for a treat: this might be all it takes to set off a cooking duel. Trying to outdo each other, they nearly always outdo themselves, and everyone wins, especially the guests or witnesses.

PETIT TRIANON DE DEGUSTATION
66, rue des Sangliers

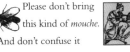 Please don't bring this kind of *mouche.* And don't confuse it with: *moche:* ugly, as in La Moche Epoque: the other side of La Belle Epoque. And here's a verbal mouthful: *amuse-gueule:* a snack, appetizer. *Gueule* is argot for face, like mug in English (*see page 58* for more on *gueule* and La Moche Epoque).

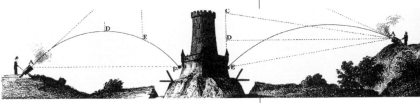

"She had the sort of beauty that was only smoldering to the touch" is a line that comes to mind for lovers who come here to stir dying embers, find old flames, or just eat some well-grilled *côtes d'agneau,* lamb chops. The décor and arrangements are very intimate, the service very discreet, the hours very late.

AUX PETITS CHARBONS ARDENTS
AT THE ARDENT LITTLE CHARCOALS
10, impasse Théodore

LA COTE D'OR
19, rue des Mauvaises
Pensées

La Côte d'Or, named for the region of which its cuisine is redolent, was closed for eight months in 1979 when the Ministère de Calembours et Jeux de Mots (Ministry of Puns and Word Play), under new directorship, took strenuous exception to its original name: *Beaune Appétit.* Acrimonious discourse, semiotic testimony, *Petit Laroussian* citations took place over splendid meals throughout the heated debates, which many Parisians came to suspect of being prolonged purely for the gastronomic pleasures of the participants. Fed up with plying his adversaries as well as his advocates with free lunches and dinners, the restaurant's proprietor threw in the towel, and his *toque,* that his daughter-in-law might fulfill her own ambitions of putting one over on the powers that be, those male chauvinistic academic *cochons,* pigs. Now she keeps a coatrack in the entranceway loaded with gold lamé wraps, which her lady diners are invited to wear at table, or, better yet, parade shamelesshussily on the sidewalk between courses, a sartorial statement calculated to offend the same *ministère,* but since *this* word play is half-English, it lies beyond its jursidiction.

Note: This restaurant review was written by a pretentious linguistic prankster terribly out of touch with humanity, but very much in touch with his uncle, a heavy shareholder in the Swiss publishing house already taking on the Italian-German-French (all in one!) Helvetican edition

of this book, so we submissively include it, but
with explanations. Beaune (pronounced *bone,*
and hence the same as in "Bon Appétit!"—the
only way to wish a person an enjoyable meal) is
a principal city in the Burgundian region of La
Côte d'Or: a good reason to visit there, no? But
all regions come to Paris, too, to cover its tables
and take its money. Well, so what about the
daughter-in-law's revenge?

Côte (slope, hill) is pronounced *coat:* that's the
English half of the pun. *D'or*—as in *doré,* not only
Gustave Doré but seen on cosmetics and tanning
lotions far from France, golden, gilded—means *of
gold.* Hence the gold lamé wraps, wrapping up
this lamentable (coerced's more like it) digression
paid for from a fat Swiss bank account.

Named for the fantastic creature in Max Ernst's
collage-novel *The Hundred Headless Woman,*
this establishment, which offers binding and gag-
ging with a surcharge, serves only after one hundred women are present, and should the number
diminish at any time, the drinks and plates cease
arriving until the number hits the mark again.
Thus trays on the way to tables often pause mid-
way, midair in fact, with a *serveur* transfixed en
route, and passing-by women are occasionally
dragged in from the sidewalk (in this case, the

BRASSERIE LOPLOP
156, rue Malentendue

 "Je suis un
homme . . . pas une
omelette."

—Anthony Burgess

With apologies to Max Ernst

binding is on the house) so a diner can make it to his box at the theater with a dinner under his belt. Naturally, this entire set-up causes rifts in friendships, courtships, and marriages, since women are suspicious of invitations, and men will go to great lengths to make it appear that this is but a passing moment in an afternoon or evening of romance, culture, and *promenades*. Transvestites are similarly in great demand, so many have made this *quartier* their home and sell their bodies (their heads, actually, since this is the part that matters, in accordance with *La Femme Cent Têtes—The Hundred Headless Woman*) at opportune moments, and rarely go hungry or unloved.

**PATTE A
LA MAIN**
PAW IN
HAND
**177, bd
des
Egyptiens**

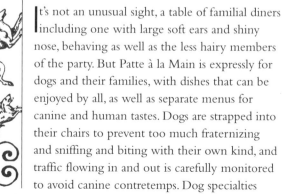

It's not an unusual sight, a table of familial diners including one with large soft ears and shiny nose, behaving as well as the less hairy members of the party. But Patte à la Main is expressly for dogs and their families, with dishes that can be enjoyed by all, as well as separate menus for canine and human tastes. Dogs are strapped into their chairs to prevent too much fraternizing and sniffing and biting with their own kind, and traffic flowing in and out is carefully monitored to avoid canine contretemps. Dog specialties include *os avec sa moelle* (bone with its marrow), *tripe à la mode de Cannis* (the canine version of *tripe à la mode de Caen,* a classic dish of Normandy), *confit de canard Canadien* (Canadian duck *confit*), *boudin Tintin* (blood sausage Tintin), *biscuits à l'aboi* (barking biscuits), and *le chien-dent* (literally dog-tooth, named for Raymond Queneau's novel of that name).

Full moon nights are reserved for wolves, and you'd be surprised how many show up. They've flown in from the Yukon, the Carcassus, the Bukovina. One such occasion was recorded and played later to a full house of poodles, who, touched by the howls, tore off their ribbons, broke out of their seat belts, disdained their *tisane*s and madeleines, and, ancient instincts aroused, proceeded to piss out their territories on the legs of the chairs and their newly estranged humans. The most instantly attracted and attuned paired off and mated for life, no need for Café Conjugal—although its proprietor, a confirmed bachelor himself, has respectfully consulted these couples when all was not going well on his premises.

 Seen in *les toilettes* at Café Nada: Lost: one *mignonne 'pattephysical* puppy, black Belgian sheepdog, intelligent (speaks, or understands, seven languages, has rudimentary grasp of typesetting). Reward. 47 77 00 95.

CANINE CAUSERIE:

☞ Would you please deliver a Grand Marnier soufflé to that charming little bitch by the window? With the compliments of my schnauzer.
✳ *Pourriez-vous servir un soufflé au Grand Marnier à cette charmante petite chienne près de la fenêtre? Avec les compliments de mon schnauzer.*

☞ One more platter of blood sausages for my bulldog, and a vegetarian pizza for me.
✳ *Une assiette de plus de boudins pour mon bulldog, et une pizza végétarienne pour moi.*

☞ My Airedale is foaming at the mouth. What did you put in his ragout?
✳ *Mon airedale bave. Qu'aviez-vous mis dans son ragoût?*

CAFE NADA
222, rue Mouquette

Besides Les Ministères, Café Nada (really a restaurant, but so called in an *aimable* attempt to balance the rocking horses at Café Dada) is another spot popular with publishers—this one with their authors and prospective ones as well, the latter favoring the Serbo-Croatian translation of *nada* as *hope,* while it's the Spanish *nothing* that's to the publishers' taste, since they have to pay for only the tables, chairs, glasses, china, silverware, and ambience—and performances of the staff.

It was actually the writers who initiated this novel approach to the publisher's lunch, suspecting that *crevette dans son coulis* (shrimp swimming in their shame) dribbling over their manuscripts and other *plats* in their plots did not add dignity to their proposals, and that a *bon mot* sometimes failed to arrive at the tip of the tongue when its mouth was crammed with *ris de veau,* veal sweetbreads. Thus arose the idea of a civilized meal with the friendly clatter of dishes, arrival of courses, banter with a witty and graceful *serveur*—and you can be sure that no *serveur* gets to work here without a solid foundation in Rabelais, Verlaine, Robbe-Grillet, Queneau, high marks in literature, and a surpassing baccalaureate. In fact, it is up to the waiters themselves to invent the literary printed menus and recite the day's specialties in the manner of Paul Valéry, Gertrude Stein, Jean Arp, Georges Perec. The best are brilliant at improvisation, serving a publisher with a menu featuring allusions to his authors, an author with allusions to his *œuvre*. Tips are on this basis, so the fellows keep up much better than the *intellos,* intellectuals, routing in Lacan and Kant. More than one *serveur,* upon retirement, has been offered a chair at the Sorbonne.

It's not easy to crash this in-world, but you might hope for a glimpse of a beloved author leaving the premises and gnawing at a stowaway *baguette* or an up-front villanelle.

If you should manage to sneak in, under true or false pretexts, be sure to use the *toilettes*. Much thought and artifice have gone into the graffiti, which the literary review *Détartine* prints whenever enough work of merit has accumulated. But this medium serves other purposes, for at times an author and his/her publisher will retire to the *toilettes* and hold spirited negotiations on the walls. Since the hand-washing part of these amenities is unisex in France, this graffiti-grappling poses no problem for mixed genders.

Naturally, books are visible in the window, and the restaurant is hung with photographs that capture famous deals made at table or behind the scenes. Agents, playing a lesser role in French literary life, are left on the sidewalk, where lavish lunches go on for days.

GLIMPSED GRAFFITI:

Authors! Beware of editor Félix Boucheloup at Pantagruel Press: He *ate* my manuscript when we met here to discuss it—then had the gall to ask our waiter to sauté the floppy disk!

Princess Hoppy is my girl.

Discreet, married publisher of a certain age seeks chilling, thrilling novella, 70 to 85 pages, which trifles with the reader's feelings, then gives him what he wants. Prefer emulation of Anatole France to parody of Raymond Roussel.

Call 43 20 79 86 for a lissome, startled sphinx with green eyes and a smart answer for every stupid question plus a truculent, monosyllabic gaucho shivering in a fat hotel—two characters who've disrupted the symmetry of my novel-in-progress, *The Stupor of Flanelle Lune.*

L'ABATOIR
45, rue des Ancians
Calomnies

Abatoirs, slaughterhouses, became all the rage after the sprawling, multisensory, hippodromiac science park La Villette was opened at the site of the old slaughterhouses north of Belleville. The architect of this ambitious project, Bernard Tschumi, is dear to the heart of this book for his remark that *Finnegans Wake* is the greatest architectural *œuvre* of the twentieth century.

L'Abatoir is a vegetarian restaurant with a flair for transmutation on the comely flanks of La Montagne Sainte-Geneviève. The name is in poor taste, but the cuisine is both imaginative and *drolatique,* to borrow an adjective from Balzac (strangely amusing, funny, even facetious). Here you may sup on stricken aubergines, asparagus cut down in the prime of life, and such dishes as *artichauts étouffés* (suffocated artichokes), *endives se reposant dans la boue* (endives resting in the mud), *haricots sous la manteau de la nuit* (beans beneath the mantle of the night), *riz basmati selon les caprices du chef* (basmati rice according to the chef's caprices), and *choc d'Alsace* (shock of Alsace)—a startling sauerkraut dish. For dessert you will be regaled by an equally vivacious chorus of sweets and treats. Not recommended is the *ossiette paysanne,* a cruel joke based on the word for plate, *assiette,* while *os* is bone; *paysanne,* peasant. Vonnegut has his admirers in France, too: each changing menu features a five-course lunch or dinner called slaughterhouse five.

BRASSERIE DES
MAUVAIS-GARÇONS
MANQUES
19, rue des Mauvais-
Garçons Manqués

In the Marais, readily happened upon as visitors at the Pompidou Center proceed to the Picasso Museum, is rue des Mauvais-Garçons, Street of the Bad Boys. Less well known is the rue des Mauvais-Garçons Manqués, where you will find two rival restaurants of the same name, each using its meaning for its own antic purposes, for *manquer* means *to miss,* and *garçon manqué* is the French term for *tomboy.* The restaurant that concerns us has waitresses dressed as male waiters, while the other is sorely missing the waiters it had when it was Le Café des Deux Hugos (the brothers being so totally unalike their mother saw no need to cast about for different names, and in accordance with the principle of opposites attracted, the two stuck together through various business ventures—but we'll find them later in *the Yellow Pages: Revenons à Nos Moutardes!).* At the first Brasserie des Mauvais-Garçons Manqués, the proprietress, chefs, dishwashers, waitresses have much in common besides thoroughly rambunctious characters, unwaxed legs, and tough cookies. All were repeatedly expelled from elementary school for carrying knives, having fist fights, breaking windows with handmade slingshots, etc., and when it came time for music lessons, they chose trombones, drums, and bass saxophones. For diners, the staff's jam sessions after hours make late dinners and long pauses through the cheese-and-cigarettes course a most rewarding dawdle.

　La carte is a saucy mixture of regional dishes and house specialties (don't miss the *rognons coup de pied,* kidneys with a kick, or the *haché aux*

A FREQUENT COMPLAINT:

🍽Our waitress just gave me a black eye and dumped this cassoulet in my lap. She also tore my stockings.

🐟*Notre serveuse m'a juste mis un œil au beurre noir et m'a renversée ce cassoulet sur mes genoux. Elle m'a aussi déchirée les bas.*

Nightly commotions sometimes swept up

troix piments, ground beef with three hot peppers), and dessert is frequently flambé. The gritty house cookie, *sablé George Sand,* is delicious with the café éclato. Do mind the cutlery: an occasional switchblade sometimes slips in, thanks to the present generation of Parisian tomboys.

Note that the restaurant is closed the first Tuesday of each month for meetings of La Société des Mauvais-Garçons Manqués—whose members, highly successful businesswomen today, cause the Mafia considerable grief.

LA PALOMA
78, rue des Regrets

The entire *carte* at La Paloma is dominated by the letter *P.* That makes for a very balanced selection, so don't write it off before pondering the possibilities: *Pain, poulet, poisson, pistou, poivron, palmier, petits pois, pissenlit, pâtes, pignons, poulpe, piperade, pistaches, pastis, pastitsio,* and, to round off the evening, *praline, profiteroles, et plein de pâtisseries.*

It somewhat spoils the effect to recite these in English, but you can't very well decide which chances to take without having a clue: Bread; chicken; fish; a Provençal basil–garlic–olive oil sauce; and soup with this as base; peppers; hearts of palm; little peas (the only kind the French will eat: adults are sent off to the salt mines);

dandelion (which in French means pissing-bed, for its diuretic properties); pasta; pine nuts; octopus; *piperade* is a Basque scrambled egg dish with peppers, tomatoes, onions, ham; pistachios; *pastis* is an anise drink; and *pastitsio* is a Greek dish with layers of macaroni, a meat and tomato and cinnamon sauce, and a very rich cheese crust on top. Let me catch my breath from this catalogue before we proceed to dessert: praline; *profiteroles* are so good I won't tell you—just order it and see for yourself!—and plenty of pastries.

If you want the inside story, a bit of gossip, you must recall Le Relais du Mois de Mai et des Muguets (see Hôtels) with that grouchy proprietress, Madame Pugnol. Monsieur Pugnol left her after thirteen unpleasant years (he took some of the cutlery to set himself up at La Paloma), and the *P* stands for his own name as well as the peace he was seeking and hoping to spread (on your *profiteroles,* for instance).

After several years as a recovering bachelor enjoying his first gulps of freedom and solitude punctuated by affairs, M. Pugnol (Ambroise to those of us who've become habitués of his dovecoted *diners*) settled down with a graduate student at the Sorbonne, Noémi Briquebout, who was soon contributing her own improvisations to the *carte* by giving La Paloma's dishes names. Among the *poissons* (fish) is her salmon in existential crisis, *saumon de Beauvoir.* Fans of

One item, since the restaurant is consecrated to *La Paix,* Peace (far though it be from the Café de la Paix on one of Paris's least peaceful corners: l'Opéra), is offered on the house: a *panaché,* or artful mix, of variegated olives rhyming with the olive branches over the door. Palomas—doves—are *not* on the menu, although they have full run of the place.

". . . Charles Baron, who has taken this stark room so as to live there with a charming girl-friend about whom I will take the liberty of saying only that on certain days she looks strangely like a stabbed dove."

—Louis Aragon

Magritte's challenges to art and reality order repeatedly the *ceci n'est pas une piperade* till the real *piperade* pipes up.

LE CADAVRE EXQUIS
9, carrefour des Mots
Croisés

Surrealist vocabulary:

hasard: The *mot juste* and *modus vivendi/operandi* of the surrealists. Not to be confused with *par hasard* (*see page 91*).

Not a den of iniquity for cannibals and necrophiliacs, Le Cadavre Exquis (with attached Caves Exquises) is an eating palace for the diner of surrealist inclination or curiosity. Based on the method of artistic collaboration that included image and words, all the dishes at this restaurant are assembled by blindfolded chefs, or *chefs d'œuvres,* who see neither their own creations nor their collaborators' work. Most dishes are the product of three or four *artistes,* although the more elaborate and expensive dishes (requiring several diners) are of more complicated genesis and expense. The chef or chefs stroll by with naked eye to see to it that the desserts are really made of sweet ingredients, and not, say, anchovies that swam over from the pizzas and canapés, but this is difficult to regulate because of how the shopping is done, also by blindfolded teams. The one guarantee by the proprietors is that all *entrées, plats, desserts* are edible and do not include mascara, sandpaper, acrylics, buckles, phantom joggers, or philosopher's stones.

CAFES: INTRODUCTION

 THE LANGUAGE OF COFFEE: *un café allongé*: a stretched-out coffee. This could mean you'll be *allongé* after drinking it, or that the caffeine has been spread out through several more cups. But if you want to amuse your waiter with your charming legs and faux paws, you could pretend to believe that a *café allongé* is to be had *à l'horizontale*. Don't try to do this "au comptoir" at the bar. A booth would be preferable, and with your Saint Bernard.

Cafés are a ubiquitous and integral part of everyday life, *la vie quotidienne*. What else could so convivially grace all those corners, sidewalks, squares? Where else could friends convene, liaisons catch on, acquaintances strike the first match? How else would you make a phone call or grope your way to the dubious *toilettes*? The *penseur/auteur* (thinker/author) Raynaud Le Blanc once declared in an interview that if he had to choose between a domicile and a favorite haunt, he'd no doubt choose the latter—in his case Le Rat Ecrémé. When his sentiments were made public, his wife and children (who didn't like him much at home anyway) sued for divorce and took away all his pocket money, so that, left with only a bank account, he had to open a café himself to pay for all his *grands crèmes* and cigarettes. You may find him up to no good, but not much mischief, either, at La Poche Déchirée, on rue des Fossés-St-Jacques—where, besides coffee and croissants, croaking monsieurs and matches, he both sells used paperback books and allows them to be written or read.

Owned and operated by the same company as Café Conditionnel, this café will not tolerate the frosty silences, whines, edges in voices married couples at times inflict upon other diners at restaurants. Thus an invitation here from one to another part of a couple on the outs immediately signals a truce: they arrive and are all charm and civility, and often forget the cause of their earlier conflict by the time they've reached the coffee and *profiteroles.* When harmonious couples come here, however, it may hail impending strife, the calm before the flames.

It is only behavior that the Café Conjugal will not tolerate. With arrangements, anything goes: a man and his dog, a woman and her mirror, a *ménage à trois* of mixed or blessed genders, the occasional dominatrix with slave. Marriage licenses are not demanded, and if they were, you can be sure the management would accept equally the certificate of *concubinage* from the *mairie.*

In the '70s and early '80s, the Conjugal surreptitiously became a bazaar for swapping partners on a short-term or permanent basis, but of course AIDS, or SIDA in French, has changed all that. So these days, it has returned to its original *raison d'être,* and unwitting diners who reproach one another or correct each other's anecdotes are forced to wash dishes, grind sausages, scrub floors, and make up while they're at it, before being sent upstairs to bed.

CAFE CONJUGAL
368, rue des Allumettes

JACQUES ROUBAUD ON THE IDEAL CROISSANT

Roubaud is one of France's greatest contemporary poets
(often quoted on pants from Arse Poetica—see Stores and Shopping),
novelists, and a professor of mathematics at University of Paris X Nanterre,
so we can be sure he's examined the croissant from all angles before coming up with his law:

The ideal croissant, . . . the croissant that might be labeled the *archetypal butter croissant,* offers the following features: a very elongated diamond, rounded at the tips but with an almost straight body (only the *plain croissant,* and it alone, has a lunar, ottomanlike look)—golden—plump—not too well done—nor too white or starchy—staining your fingers through the India paper that wraps, or rather holds it together—still warm (from the oven it has just recently left, it has not yet cooled) . . .

It has three principal components, and three interlocking meaty compartments protected by a tender shell that lends it certain similarities to a young lobster. The center section is, in this croissant-lobster homomorphism, the body of the crustacean; the end parts are the pincerless claws. It's an extremely stylized lobster, a *formal lobster,* in short. For the croissant to be perfect, a simple tug on each "claw" should easily pull them apart from the "body," each trailing along an oblique, tapering excrescence of inner meat, subtracted from the center, extracted, as it were, effortlessly from the still very warm innards of the croissant, without making crumbs, or any sound, or rips. I openly lay claim to the discovery of this correspondence, this structural morphism (at least I have found no "plagiarism by anticipation") which I propose calling *Roubaud's Law of Butter Croissants.*

—Jacques Roubaud

Many conjectures have been offered for the origin of the art movement's name: Russian for "Yes yes" is controversial, as they were saying "NO" to quite a few things too—all the conventions of art and life, including war and logic. Café Dada has thrown in its lot with the rocking-horse meaning of the word and furnished its famished premises accordingly. Here the tablecloths are of the best lace and the chairs are shaped like rocking horses. They move like them too, which gives customers something to do while awaiting the waiters and considering the *carte*, or menu. But there are no menus, or waiters; nor is there even a kitchen. The west wall is lined with a row of food and drink machines, into which clients feed unwanted food, coffee, and hot chocolate (from other restaurants, hotel breakfasts, friends' supper parties, customers' own *salles à manger*, dining rooms). In return the machines give back a variety of overseas coins. Eating and drinking is strictly forbidden on the premises. A visit to Café Dada goes very nicely with a night or two at Hôtel Triana, where the management has not lost its childlike wonder and its endearing rebelliousness.

CAFE DADA
7, impasse de Fantômas

WARNING! The machines in this establishment have been known to behave abusively if they are plied with *bouffe*, grub, not to their taste. On one occasion a machine was taken to court for spitting a dubious lukewarm liquid back at a customer. However, it was judged that the act was not malicious but random (hence qualifying it as a Dadaist statement in full compliance with the café's manifesto).

For Sale: 1 cigar box of the finest Cuban adjectives, nightclubs, and imbroglios. B.P. 178, 75003 Paris. No Russian or Cuban coins accepted—unless, of course, you want to coin a phrase.

CAFE TREPAN
22, rue de la Carpe

"[Scobie] spoke indifferent English and French, but whenever at loss for a word he would put in one whose meaning he did not know and the grotesque substitution was often delightful. This became his standard mannerism. In it, he almost reached poetry—as when he said . . . 'The car is trepanned today' . . ."

—Lawrence Durrell

The English owner of this café, a former medical historian, came up with the name in the hopes that it would symbolize a place where the after-work crowd could relieve the pressures of their busy lives. Little did he realize that not only have most English speakers forgotten that to be trepanned is to have a hole drilled into your head, but to French speakers it somehow suggests having a car break down—that is, to be *en panne* (or, if you want to be really correct, *être en panne*). So, this being Paris, Café Trépan has turned into a magnet for car mechanics and taxi drivers who have heard about it by word of mouth and who undoubtedly have never seen the name spelt out (the sign is rather too high above eye level)—although why they would go to a place that implied mechanical failure is anybody's guess. Great fun when the taxi companies' shifts change and drivers from the rival Ça va Chauffer! and Auto da Fée arrive: the sparks fly as well as the fur.

Facing the kitchen hangs the well-known photo of Guillaume Apollinaire, his war-wounded head bandaged, with a caption from his own poem:

"Wounded in the head trepanned under chloroform"

Redolent of both the fragrance frangipani and the pastry frangipane, Café Frangipane is an all-around dessert, delight, and debauch salon, with guests' senses, and their indulgence, most on the management's minds. Its *carte* offers not specific *pâtisseries,* drinks, *délices,* but categories, and *canapés* (an item of furniture, a sofa, not a bite of bread topped with a snail or laughing cow) on which they are toyed with, nibbled, and sipped, sometimes in a swoon.

Lalique
Tonique
Pique-nique
Tropique
Nomadique

Those ordering the *Lalique* must pay for insurance as well as the privilege of drinking from and eating off Lalique crystal: the insurance is included in the price, and the pastries are as exquisite as the glasses, plates, and Lalique vases holding frangipani flowers, roses, and other seasonal or hothouse flowers. The *Tonique* delivers a wallop of well-being, a mini-fountain-of-youth, bracing you for the now with intimations of immortality. After the sweet recline, *Toniqueurs* and *Toniqueuses* often sprint out of the place and head for the Bois de Boulogne. The *Pique-nique,* picnic, is just what it says, a casual sprawl with a wicker basket on the roll-out lawn, the fare and china less fragile than the other choices here.

CAFE FRANGIPANE
58, rue Barbarie

THE LANGUAGE OF GLASS:
un verre: A glass, or first move, often from a total stranger, as in "Voulez-vous prendre un verre avec moi?" Reply: "Dommage, mais j'ai déjà pris un joli verre avec les polonnais" ("Sorry [or tough luck], but I've already had a lovely glass with the Poles"). But if you stay long enough to start recording things in your pocket calendar/diary, you will soon be entering such notes as "Heloïse verre vers 16 h."
vers: toward, or just about (also *à peu près*)

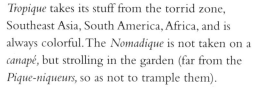"The café was sparkling. Even its gas lights displayed all the fervor of an opening, and at full blast they illumined the blindingly white walls, the mirror's dazzling expanses, the gilding of the moldings and cornices, the chubby-cheeked pages dragged about by leashed dogs, the ladies laughing at the falcon perched on their fist, the nymphs and goddesses carrying fruits, pâtés, and game on their heads, the Hebes and Ganymedes presenting with outstretched arms little amphoras of mousse or bicolored obelisks of blended ice creams. All history and all mythology at the command of gluttony."
—Charles Baudelaire

Tropique takes its stuff from the torrid zone, Southeast Asia, South America, Africa, and is always colorful. The *Nomadique* is not taken on a *canapé,* but strolling in the garden (far from the *Pique-niqueurs,* so as not to trample them).

Toxique, a clandestine choice and very dear, is only for suicides and *crimes passionnels*—but for this, arrangements must be made ahead of time, with the *Pompes Funèbres* (pompous funerals) as well as the chef.

Customers recline and sit on silk cushions and are served by waiters in silk pajamas. A boutique next door sells the pajamas, or for 20 francs, you may rent a pair till you leave. It's worth the price just for a visit to the dressing room. The Frangipane is a heady mélange of nineteenth-century Orientalism, a touch of Flaubert's fantasy *Salammbô,* and *The Rubaiyat of Omar Khayyam,* but somehow it all works, and the pleasures are so subtle we'd do them a disservice by trying to put them into words.

Thé de Ceylan, a *salon de thé* (tea room), began as a place to get hopped up on the caffeine of the camellia leaf, but changing times, consciousness, and ownership (it's now run by a runaway from an ashram in County Cork, who used to be a disk jockey on Dublin's "Celtic Twilight") have brought with them not only a flavor of Celtic mists and mysticism, but also *tisanes* of medicinal herbs and aromatics you have to take your chances with: they do vary from day to day and have an awesome ability to affect your mood. New Age literature in many languages lines one wall of bookshelves and magazine racks, and Wednesday nights feature a speaker, phenomenon, or visitant, with mass ecstasy afterward. If you can bear the bliss (not bad when it's not too smug), this is a place where you can check out a lot of the New Age musicians who've caused so much grief to record stores, the way these records spill over into Jazz, Pop, World Music, even classical besides the soporific sounds in orbit from the Heart of Space. As for the tea itself, here *infusion* is just what it says: you *will* walk away infused, suffused, to the last delicate drop—emitting scents of petals from the world over till your next steak tartare.

THE DE CEYLAN
20, rue Charlotte Corday

AUX DEBOIRES DE PETROUCHKA
48, rue Jonquille

Here you can eat *zakuska* with your vodka (pink, yellow, white) just like Stravinsky often did and listen to music that will stir your soul and make your toeshoes twitch.

[123] A note à la mode: It was the Ballets Russes, so Karl Lagerfeld explains, that brought color to Paris fashion, women wearing only black, white, muted shades of blue, gray, and pink before this explosion of music, movement, backgrounds, costumes, and *beaux gestes*.

Petrouchka does drink a lot here, and so do his guests, who are waited on by somewhat out-of-work *corps de ballet* dancers with exquisite turn-outs and pelvic girdles that make their service a pleasure to behold. Since this is a ballet bar, barres do indeed line one wall, and are used by the waiters in spare moments between orders and *pourboires,* tips.

Déboire means aftertaste, and figuratively vexation or disappointment, so customers come before or after and taste whatever they want or can get of a nighttime's possibilities. But remember this is named for Petrouchka, that so very human puppet in the Stravinsky-Fokine ballet, come to life only to fall in love and be humiliated by a swaggering swain. No wonder we weep for him, are frightened for him, identify with him when we're down. Thus, some come here to celebrate their good fortunes, others to drown their sorrows. For everyone, something changes while they're clowning around. One corner is reserved for more sober pursuits: several serious card games played against the backdrop of a large photo blow-up: Stravinsky and Balanchine at their own *Jeu de Cartes* (which was one of their loveliest, most modern ballets).

This nightclub/bar is a monument, in its own way, to Diaghilev and his Ballets Russes,[123] and the richly colored and textured décor recalls the productions that shook up society when they first were danced.

SERVICES

"I wanted to know if there still existed in his domain a bizarre establishment which Valéry had once described to me: an agency which accepted unstamped letters and arranged to have them posted from any desired point of the globe to the address written on the envelope, a facility that would allow the customer to feign a voyage to the far east, for example, without moving an inch from the far west of some secret adventure."

—Louis Aragon

Are you exasperated with fellow travelers, with the compromises that must be made over every stop and start of the day? Do you long for solitary adventures, sleazy or *haute culture?* Are you simply too polite, timid, phony to just say so and strike out on your own? Le Service Kidnapping will swiftly rescue and misplace you, discretion assured. Since they have their hands full *en pleine saison,* the less self-deceiving travelers make tentative arrangements well in advance, to within the week of probable restlessness.

LE SERVICE KIDNAPPING
158, rue des Escroqueries

"Save me from my friends."
—Voltaire

CHACUN A SON GOUTEUR

A tasting service by accredited members of the Association de Gastronomie et Manger (a division of the Musée de Gastronomie Mais Pas Dégustation). For a nominal fee it can be arranged that members will taste your drinks or meals to prevent untimely or unsightly deaths from deliberate or accidental poisonings. Specializing in arsenic, cyanide, and everyday ptomaine. Particularly adept with steak tartare, be it *boeuf* or *cheval.* Given their political and ideological mandate, don't expect these gastronomers to stand by at the Café Dada. You must provide your own credenza.

LE SERVICE PRE-GOUTER
10, voie Unique

To each his own taster, which isn't really true, although if you are pleased with a particular individual, you may request him/her again and hope he/she is still alive.

Le Service Pré-Goûter was established in Italy in 1503, the year the Borgias infamously poisoned Cardinal Giovanni Michiel of Venice.

THE FRENCH POSTAL SYSTEM
La Poste et ex-Communications at Le Pont Traversé

EX-COMMUNICATIONS:

☞Do you have a ladder so I can reach your air-mail clerk suspended from the ceiling?

◉*Avez-vous une échelle ainsi je pourrai atteindre votre employé de la poste aérienne qui est suspendu du plafond?*

☞I wish to send this to my cousin in Zurich. It's not a letter—it's just torn paper in the style of Jean Arp. Is it the same rate?

◉*Je souhaite envoyer ceci à mon cousin à Zurich. Ce n'est pas une lettre—c'est juste un papier déchiré dans le style Jean Arp. Est-ce le même prix?*

The brutality and surliness of the French postal system are familiar to travelers and inhabitants alike, although the visitor whose rhino hide has many layers yet to grow is more likely, after the simplest transaction, to go off whimpering into several glasses of pastis or cassis. La Poste et ex-Communications facing the Surrealist bookstore Le Pont Traversé, however, has special disservices of its own. Letters mailed from this *poste,* whose employees are suspended from the ceiling in mockery of airmail transport and the Surrealist Map of the Heavens, are delivered only to the countries and cities that show on the Surrealist Map of the World. Thus the girl from La Rochelle, on the French coast, filialpietously sending home a postcard of *La Dame aux Licornes* to her *maman,* is out of luck, *la chance,* for the delivery of mail from this *poste* is anything but *par hasard,* since France is nothing but Paris (see detail of map), which puts her mother's lap in the sea, which has swallowed up the rest of France. La Poste Transversée, as the locals and literati call it, is popular with tropical islanders, resplendently noted by the mad cartographer, or those whose own countries are unmapped and who've thus adopted relatives in the Pacific to have someone to regale with their *cartes postales.* For Americans, it's a great relief, their expatriation complete, and lately, now the curtain's down, Russian *babas* receive packets of letters meant for all the mothers of the world otherwise out of reach. Many *babas* trade these packets with Russian gangsters for a ticket to visit the French Impressionists at the Hermitage.

For your vocabulary:

par hasard: by accident as opposed to *exprès:* on purpose (*see page 76*).

With apologies to *The Surrealist Map of the World* (detail)

BUREAU DES BOULEVERSEMENTS
4, Grand Etoile des Cauchemars

An item for your vocabulary: *bouleversé:* overwhelmed, bowled over. Once familiar with this word you'll use it everywhere.

Twenty-four-hour (*24 sur 24*) multilingual weather reports available by calling your hotel reception desk or the Bureau des Bouleversements. Allow twenty-four hours for a response if calling the latter.

▼

Since *le Maire* Pierrot le Fou took up residency and majesty at the Hôtel de Ville, tourists receive gentler handling on a totally unpredictable basis. One day it's abuse and scoffing, yet another it's all kid gloves and *bonhomie*. Still, certain bureaucratic niches were hollowed out and filled with occasional *sympathie*. One of the most needed, scattered, and called-upon is the network of crisis centers established for travelers who are *bouleversés* by the *grands boulevards*. This might sound superfluous from where you're comfortably seated, your map in your lap, but just wait 'til you try cutting straight through a nexus where six or eight boulevards meet, especially if you have some place in mind that you're going or a hot date with a sphinx in high heels: you're likely to lose not only your way but the name of the *rue* or *boulevard* and its chosen direction by the time you've saved your own life from at least one Renault or Peugeot.

On an inclement day they may do little but spin you around and toss you out in the traffic again, but usually the traumatized are soothed and reoriented in line with the particular center's policies and the *quartier*'s quirks, as well as the talents of the oft-turned-over staff (mostly men and women in training for taxi-driving). This is also a fine place to meet fellow travelers and exchange itineraries—sometimes literally.

How far these establishments have come from the *blanchisseries* of Victor Hugo's day! Now, with *laveries* brightening the corners, it's every sock for itself, very self-service, with evening hours and coins. Long ago, the poor girls who did others' laundry could barely feed and clothe themselves without a bit of prostitution on the side, and *quelle chance* if you were pretty, had nice ankles or a creamy neck. Many Parisians and some visitors send out a parcel of laundry here and there—but self-service machinery is also at your behest. Go to the photogenic Blanchisserie Chérubini at Square Louvois with your camera, but for good clean fun with dirty *chemises,* seek out the *laverie* most convenient to your Paris address. With its cute one-legged, two-wheeled carts and can't-beat-it-location, the Julice on rue Monsieur-le-Prince is a paragon of working order and sound sense. You deposit your laundry in the machine of your choice, then deposit your money in a central bank. Payment made, punching the number of your particular Miele machine activates its leisurely one-hour cycle. This gives you time to walk your eyes through the Moniteur bookstore and various publishers' showrooms in the neighborhood, or sprint to a nearby sprawl, for the Julice is situated equidistant from Le Jardin du Luxembourg, the cafés at la place de la Sorbonne, and the soft stone steps of l'Odéon.

LAUNDROMATS/ LAVERIES

Many *laveries* include a *nettoyage à sec*—dry cleaning—machine with signs strictly forbidding its use for throw rugs, curtains, upholstery, and domestic animals, so you'd be wise to wash your Labradors and ocelots in your hotel's *salle de bain.*

LE MONITEUR/ JULICE

"[Oscar Wilde] was walking home through the Paris streets. Crossing the Pont des Arts, he stopped to look at the green water rivering enticingly below. Suddenly he noticed a poorly dressed man near him, also looking down at the river. 'Hein, mon pauvre, êtes-vous désespéré?' he asked. 'Non, monsieur,' came the answer, 'je suis coiffeur.' 'Hey, my poor man, are you desperate?' 'No, sir, I'm a hairdresser.' "

—Richard Ellmann

LE PETIT ENFER
12, rue des Anges
Rouges

If it's other kicks you're after while losing the inevitable sock, you shouldn't miss either La Slaverie with its signs in Cyrillic and its dreadful Russian soap or the laundrette all Chinoiserie now attached to La Pagode (see Nightlife and Entertainment, *Cinémas*), where you can watch continually playing shorts while your own shorts are coming clean. At La Slaverie, by the way, only the machine is your slave, just like the Constructivists expected before history Stalinized their dreams.

Salle Japonaise in La Pagode

Note: The Salle Japonaise has lots of waves for washing on the ceiling, a man with umbrella, so this is where the management got the idea of the *laverie.*

n another *quartier* entirely, quite a cut below, at 12 rue des Anges Rouges, is Le Petit Enfer—*ouvert 24 sur 24,* twenty-four hours a day. The dryers have *gueules diaboliques,* diabolical faces, and can blaze the moisture out of any pillowcase, sheet, towel, rug in three minutes flat. Since the washers take an eternity, however, the management has kindly provided its doomed clientele with several *divertissements.* The change machines double as slot machines; press one button *et voilà*—instant casino! There's also an endless poker game going on in one corner, but any stripping is strictly at your discretion, as the *joueurs,* players, are usually half-dressed, anyway, while their underpants, T-shirts, blouses, *pantalons* are having the purgatorial time of their lives with the softener and soap. The decks of cards are like no others—medieval woodcut skeletons and dancers of death in various states of undress—and can be purchased at Une Saison en Enfer, beside the Catacombs, place Denfert Rochereau, or from souvenir/concession stands in all the major cemeteries of La Ville de Paris. It may be hard to find, or rather notice, the latter, as they are nearly indistinguishable from the mausoleums.

This is a service that only Paris could offer, with her philosophers elevated to star status and her epistemological cigarettes. The usual practice is to meet at the appropriate café and to be lost in your thoughts as you arrive. English speaking is extra, as are the Eastern philosophers, who will also check your breathing and the state of your soul. The regular guy, Joe Blow (Jacques Tacques) specialties include: Lacanian, Bergsonian, Freud mit Toast, Aurobindian, Oblomovesque, Pat-apoufian, ErikSatieque (see Sights, *Churches*),

PHILOSOPHE A L'HEURE
58, rue Cassetou

"My voice is your voice and
     you recognize
My will. But you want . . .
     ME! The Idea!"
                    —Paul Valéry

Derridada, 'Pataphysical, Existentialiste, Alchimique (includes, for 15,000 F, a digression on *le mystère des cathédrales Gothiques,* or, for 1,500 F, a tour of the alchemical symbols on doors in the Marais—not covered at Musée de la Porte, so don't think you'll get it that way), Franchement Nihiliste, and many mongrels thereof. Ubu impersonators are not welcome at most cafés, so separate arrangements must be made if you wish to drench yourself in their colorful language.

LE FAX FOOD
55, rue des
Ambassades
Inconnues

Le Fax Food is a *traiteur* specializing in fax packs of *délices* and *friandises,* as well as more substantial meals if you subscribe to their service described below. The customer, for instance, in Helsinki, Kyoto, or Vancouver receives *un grand crème* with croissant (in pure accordance with Roubaud's *Law of Butter Croissants,* right down to the tender tug of its claws, see page 80) on paper and translates it into substance when *appétit* is aroused. Faxes obeying their own laws (speed, that is), this usually happens *tout de suite,* all the more so because the items are written with such delectable precision that only the fiercest anorexic could hold out for long. If you have a fax built into your computer, you can print it out or go directly for transubstantiation with the cuisine attachment (sold only by Le Fax Food) that you install at the side of your monitor.

Le Fax Food also has a remarkable culinolinguistic capacity, translating a meal from another country (German, English, to name two much-maligned cuisines) into its French refinement. *Hasenpfeffer* from Dresden, to take the Teutonic example, makes its strange journey through Le Fax Food and comes out kicking its rabbit legs as *lapin à Gilles. Kalbshaxe,* which sounds like a hoof to eat with an ax, is transformed into the more inviting traditional French *blanquette de veau.* Not the even more inviting *banquette de veau,* a bench of veal, which was featured at Le Musée de Gastronomie Mais Pas Dégustation during an exciting collaboration between regional charcuteries and furniture fabricators. There have been allegations that Ministère de Culture funds are being faxed over to this service, right into its bank account: shady deals between government officials, museum curators, and Le Fax Food entrepreneurs. All of them are looking for ways to prolong their pleasures at table, in their offices even. International scandal may be coming with future revelations, once the revelers are caught with napkins on and licking their machines during working hours.

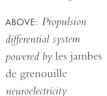

ABOVE: *Propulsion differential system powered by* les jambes de grenouille *neuroelectricity*

TOILETTES POUR LES FEMMES

Toilettes pour les femmes facilities can easily be recognized by this handy universal symbol

Visiting *les toilettes* (cheerfully announced as open by a sign outside, "Les toilettes sont ouvertes") at Le Jardin du Luxembourg is always a pleasant experience. The attendant, with proud bearing and smoothly coiffed hair, makes you feel most welcome, as if you'd dropped in for tea. The small facilities gleam with her care, while the hand-towel is the sort you'd buy in quantity if you were opening your own *trattoria.*

While some of us are squatting over Turkish toilets trying not to piss on our stockings and panties, ankles and socks, the pampered sybarites pee in style. Mocking the *châlets d'aisance*—chalets of relief—or *pissoirs* of old, these exclusive *toilettes*—many in *places* and squares embroidered with flowers—await their well-heeled customers for whom this is as *agréable* an outing as the day's rendezvous at a *salon de thé.*

Here the music playing is often from the Court of Bourbon or the heavenly voices of William Christie's *Les Arts Florissants,* and the décor inspired by L'Ecole de Fontainebleau—lots of flesh, cupid and human, voluptuous and *en déshabille.* The *papier de toilette* changes daily, from vanilla-scented to jasmine, rose, mandarin. You might begin to wonder, if you wander into one of these outrages with your 85 F, if you're not at the ice cream stand with its praline, lime, nougat, and chocolate cones. Here you may dawdle, if there's not a line (too many women having consumed too much champagne or sauternes with their oysters) and admire your thighs or go over the day's agenda yet to untwine. This system of *toilettes de luxe* is another brainchild of the societies that furnished Métro Récamier, and here the profits go to buy notebooks and sketchbooks, pens and paintbrushes for the langoustically and linguistically deprived students of the shabbier primary and junior high schools.

The rest of us, for whom the franc tip at Café de Cluny or the coin-operated *toilettes* are cause for indignation, may heed a few notes for the *toilettes ordinaires.* If you enter a booth and find it dark, all you have to do is fumble around for the lock on the door. Cranked into place, this delivers your share of both light and privacy. If shocking your hands with a blast of hot air after such delicate operations is not what you wanted, take some toilet paper with you as you approach the sink. Even the most civilized-looking brasserie can catch you off-guard with a Turkish toilet downstairs, so be prepared to swish your skirts out of the way, and if you're wearing tights, well, *bonne chance,* good luck. They're superfluous indoors, anyway, as you may have noticed in the last waiting room or métro car (we're talking winter here) and you should have taken them off long ago. The *toilettes* at the Brasserie du Louvre are quite nice, and you can enter any lavish restaurant and say you must use *les toilettes* before contemplating *la carte.* Strange things go on in the *toilettes* at Beaubourg—you may encounter voyeurs with the most original methods of looking up your legs.

"A mauve sky, which the illuminations filled with something like the glow of an enormous fire—the sound of countless footsteps creating the effect of the rushing of great waters—the crowds all black, that reddish, burnt-paper black of present-day crowds—a sort of intoxication on the faces of the women, many of whom were queuing up outside the lavatories, their bladders bursting with excitement—the place de la Concorde an apotheosis of white light, in the middle of which the obelisk shone with the rosy colour of a champagne ice—the Eiffel Tower looking like a beacon left behind on earth by a vanished generation, a generation of men ten cubits tall."

—Edmond and Jules
de Goncourt

Mauvaise position

Tombeau de l'Emp

DROIT D'ENTRÉE
pour la visite du Tombeau de l'Empereur

A conserver par le visiteur
pour être présenté à toute réquisition

CONTR

FRANCE PANORAMIQUE

P

SIGHTS

"In the raw veiled spring morning faint odours float of
morning Paris: aniseed, damp sawdust, hot dough of
bread; and as I cross the Pont Saint Michel the steel blue
waking waters chill my heart. . . .Tawny gloom in the
vast gargoyled church."

—James Joyce

N° D'ORDRE
SUR LA LISTE
D'ÉMARGEMENT

2ᵉTⁿ49 2ᵉTⁿ49 2ᵉTⁿ49 2ᵉTⁿ49 2ᵉTⁿ49
33 32 31 30 29 28
A A A A A

BABY
CH

RÉUNION

TOURING

FONDÉ EN 1890

Mr G Bart
21 rue de É

LE PRÉSIDENT

Adhérez à l'Association
Les Monuments Historiques de la France

les Tuileries

SEINE

du Louvre

d'Orsa

N° 401,984

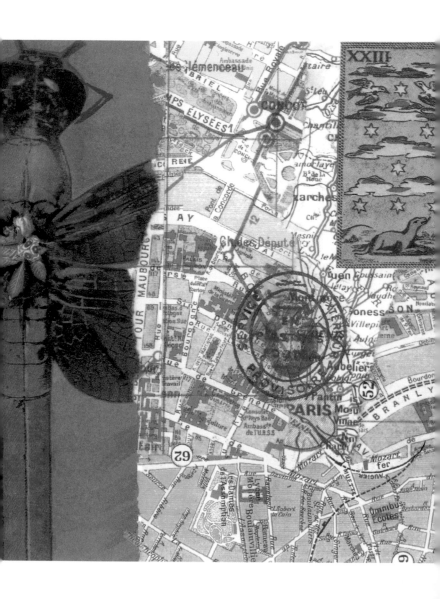

"And that! over there!! Look!!! The Panthéon!!!!"

"Tisn't the Panthéon," said Charles, "it's the
    Invalides. . . ."

"Oh go on," cried Gabriel, "so that isn't the
    Panthéon?"

"No, it's the Invalides," replied Charles. . . .

"Are you sure about that," he asks him, "are you
    really so sure as all that?"

Charles didn't answer.

"What is there that you're absolutely sure
    about?" Gabriel insisted.

"I've got it," Charles then roars, "that thing
    there, tisn't the Invalides it's the Sacré-Coeur."

"And you I suppose," says Gabriel jovially,
    "wouldn't by any chance be the sacred cow?"
                        —Raymond Queneau

**THE PANTHEON, NO,
THE INVALIDES . . .**

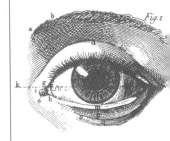

What do Tour St-Jacques and Balzac's Passy
pavilion have in common? A butcher. Not
the same butcher (many centuries apart), but
of blood brotherhood, as the full name of the
sixteenth-century church that once stood here is
Saint-Jacques-de-la-Boucherie. If it's butchers
you're really interested in, there's a very handsome one on rue Rambuteau. There's also a
butchers' ballet in a novel by Blaise Cendrars,
which bears mention here because the bar
where the brawl takes place is—*oh la la!*—La

**TOUR SAINT-
JACQUES**

**BALZAC'S
HOUSE**

"The tower of Saint-Jacques
    in Paris totters
Like a sunflower
Bumps its brow a bit on the
    River Seine then its
    shadow goes
    slipping off snugly
    among the tugboats"
        —André Breton

Taupinière. No relation to the respectable hotel chain by the RER (although the suburbs can be quite rough and rife in drugs, gangsters, and phone booths used for illegal purposes, so you might want to keep a butcher's knife on you when you stay there, all the same).

"It was just striking three. The Taupinière *had barely opened and already you could hardly get in, just like every night, there were butchers, citizens, drivers, carmen, swankers, lushes and quite a bit of young stuff and ass. . . . I finished one glass, another, a third, a fourth, laughing to myself, biding my time, looking at the mugs on all of them and enjoying myself hugely for there's always a hell of a shindy at the* Taupinière *and the kind of arguments and wisecracking and scrapping I like goes on there all the time. . . . Pow! Have that, you old swine, and all of a sudden it's a brawl, you'd think the crowd was waiting for nothing else but that, to start jumping on each other and bashing each other about fit to wreck the joint. . . . One type was soaking starched serviettes in the sauces and mayonnaise and hurling handfuls of them into the mêlée. Talk about a brawl! What with the butchers who'd taken the bar by storm under the pretext of helping the owner, but were really looting it and stripping it, beating each other over the head like Punch and Judy with salamis they'd unhooked from the ceiling at the back, you'd have thought it was a massacred wedding*

party what with their bonnets and their white aprons all smeared with the blood of the abattoirs."

—Blaise Cendrars

But it's time to turn to more delicate matters, the matter of Balzac's feminine identity. Following the ruination of his pineapple farms and printing enterprises, Balzac hid from his creditors at a charming pavilion (owned by a butcher) in Passy under the name of his governess, Madame de Breugnol. When his friends came to visit, they had to ask for him by this name *and* had to dress up as women themselves, announced with appropriately feminine names. George Sand could do as she pleased in name and dress, and was so confused that she rarely paid a call. In 1985 Le Musée de la Mode et du Costume mounted a special exhibition featuring these disguises—one of their most heavily attended shows. The opening astounded its stellar guests with the Monty Python players in drag, who decided with difficulty which female characters should come, but of course the pair that had set out from a London laundrette and crossed the English Channel to talk fine points of philosophy with Jean-Paul Sartre were among those on hand for the gala cross-dressing *soirée*.

"Open wide your peepers, clots and clotesses," said Fyodor Balanovitch. "On

You really should visit Balzac's house (47, rue Raynouard) to cool your heels in placid Passy—once a village (Balzac had to ferry to Paris, in fact), now an elegant neighborhood—not only for Madame de Breugnol's almost sylvan backdrop, the character charts of *La Comédie Humaine,* and Balzac's beloved coffee pot, but also to touch the sky and buildings as the métro suddenly rises above ground and drifts westward above the avenues.

your right you are about to see the Gare d'Or-
say. It's very in-te-res-ting, architecturally, and
it'll make up for the Sainte-Chapelle, if we
arrive too late . . ." . . .

"Sainte-Chapelle," they tried to say. "Sainte-
Chapelle."

"Yes yes," he said amiably. "The Sainte-Chapelle
(silence) (gesture) that gem of Gothic art
(gesture) (silence)."

"Don't start talking crap all over again," said
Zazie sourly.

"Go on, go on," cried the travellers, drowning
the child's voice. "We want to hearken, we want
to hearken," they added in a great berlitzcoulian
effort.

—Raymond Queneau

PARC CHAUVE-SOURIS

❄Do you come to this
noctambupark often? Are
the bats given annual
rabies shots?

☞ *Venez-vous souvent à ce
noctambuparc? Est-ce que les
chauves-souris reçoivent leurs
piqûres de rage annuelle?*

Formerly Parc Montsouris, until a blight of
Transylvanian provenance attacked the *mont,*
mound/mount, and all its foliage, and left it
embarrassed and bald. It has since become rough
and ababble with brooks and grottoes and is
today a favorite haunt of bats, flattered, no
doubt, by the new name. Unlike other parks in
La Ville de Paris system, Parc Chauve-Souris
opens at sundown and stays that way till dawn. It
may help you to get oriented here if you understand that *souris* means *mouse,* while *chauve-souris,*

literally *bald mouse,* is French for *bat.* The Rumanians who have a fine restaurant near the Rumanian Embassy on avenue de la Bourdonnais and rue Saint Dominique (practically at the feet of the Eiffel Tower) moved in swiftly here (with a concession on the grounds) to open another place serving Rumanian herbed goat cheese, *ghivetch,* a Rumanian stew with every vegetable that could possibly grow in Balkan soil, and other specialties of the former Dacia.[63] Ghivetch usually calls for an entire head of garlic, but the chef had to tone this down to the barest whisper, as it frightened away the bats and all the tourists coming in the hopes of an encounter with Count Dracula and his long-toothed groupies.

[63]*Dacia* is the ancient name of Rumania.

"Grey against grey, the statues sunned themselves in the still shrouded gardens. In the long parterres, here and there single flowers stood up and said 'Red' with a frightened voice."

—Rainer Maria Rilke

LES CHENES ANDALOUS

Parc les Chênes Andalous turns the *chien,* dog, of the movie title *Le Chien Andalou* into a tree, as *chêne* is French for *oak.* This is a scruffy place festooned with oak trees from Andalusia and habitually crawling with flies. It's not safe at certain times, but as these times are never the same, you'd best come with your wolf or bodyguard or park your fetching form beside a *citoyen vénérable,* venerable citizen, although not many of them come here these days.

CREDIT EGYPTIEN
104, avenue des Grands Chameaux

A few translations to help you negotiate the complicated automatic teller. All bankcards are accepted:

GIVE!

OKAY

TODAY'S DATE

URGENT!

WHAT IS YOUR NAME?

YES

YOU ARE THE OWNER OF THE GOLD

You could do worse than the lobby of the Crédit Egyptien if you need a place to rest your feet and find relief—bas-relief, that is. This bank is on the same side of the avenue as the Gare Luxor, from which the spontaneous *Aïda* processions sometimes depart.

Bas-reliefs on the interior walls show such historical figures as Marat, Charlotte Corday, Louis XVIII, Cardinal Richelieu, Madame de Pompadour, Napoléon, and Charles de Gaulle in typical early Egyptian profile or seated on thrones with their salukis nearby, while changing displays of written language remind us that the art of the cartoon, or *bande dessinée,* goes back to the time of the Great Sphinx. Of special allure is the cat mummy, *la momie d'un chat,* with his whiskers and fixed-forever stare. But this is the only place, the bank claims, where you'll also see the cat mummy's own mummy of a mouse, and the mouse's mummy of Mimolette, a cheese so hard it almost mummifies itself. You can find this cheese in most eclectically stocked *fromageries.*

With the telecommunication changes sweeping the globe, the Crédit Egyptien is announcing its own innovations: an automatic teller system in hieroglyphics. When you open an account here, you are given a multilinguistic dictionary to tell you what each hieroglyphic button and message or dialogue box means so your requests will be symbolically correct.

As you know, Le Service Pré-Goûter is not offered for Patte à la Main, but if your dog should die in Paris from too much rich food or excitement, you can bury him in the dog cemetery, the Cimetière des Chiens, in Asnières near the banks of the Seine. Although the model for Proust's Baron de Charlus, Comte Robert de Montesquiou, described himself as "a greyhound in a greatcoat," he is not buried here, and although cats prefer to keep their distance from dogs, Inspector Clouseau's animated pink panther *is*. It died from an abscess that got out of hand in one paw following a scuffle over some stolen diamonds and furs.[327] The funeral was a touching spectacle, all sorts of celebrities paying their last respects, from Yves St-Laurent to Rudolf Nureyev.

Wolves sometimes like to have their ashes scattered in La Vallée aux Loups, the Valley of the Wolves, where Châteaubriand's house is open to visitors during visiting hours, as it was once very much open *all* the time to Madame Récamier. Ashes, ashes, falling down, but not from the Eiffel Tower. Although there are a few costly crypts partway up the Eiffel Tower, the fine for scattering your other best friend's cremains from its heights is 20,000 francs, and the misbehaving mourner may not enter the city for five years from the moment of his/her offense.

LE CIMETIERE DES CHIENS

(closed Tuesdays and holidays)

[327] the panther was after the furs, Clouseau was after the diamonds

ASHES IN TODAY'S COSMOPOLIS

A CONCESSIONNAIRE GIVES UP THE GHOST

You see that sign there? About what it takes to ensure oneself a plot in perpetuity here? There's more than plots of earth in this place—plots of stories, too. The things I've seen and heard! I'm just waking up, so excuse me if my thoughts are a bit disjointed. The joints of my bones are becoming unattached as well, hardly unexpected after my one hundred and sixty years as a corpse. Oh, I was an exquisite cadaver. I remember my daughters, no better at housework than I (and apparently this defect has worked its way down through the generations, which is why I'm being booted out: no one has tended my slab, moss, and *myrtilles*—such a conventional plant for the likes of me), saying how beautiful I looked in my rubies, ballgown, my favorite wig, my shoes of Spanish leather brought back by an admirer after a visit to the Roi de Sicile. Well, why shouldn't I have looked my best at the moment of my death, in the midst of an orgy at the place des Vosges (I always did have a weak heart), still quite fresh and frisky for a countess of my age. A countess, I said, so of course I had servants and could be slovenly whenever and however I wished. The cemetery, though, is a different matter, but I will not leave before indulging in a few reminiscences about my tenure here.

You do know, of course, that Père Lachaise was named for Louis XIV's confessor, who once farmed this land. I remember when Molière was brought over to add a bit of class, as if a literary salon would soon be in full swing. We let him keep to himself for a while, to savor once again the irony of his demise during *Le Malade Imaginaire*. I've witnessed many arrivals since my own, but none was more disturbing than that of the last 147 Communards to die— slaughtered and dumped all together in the southwest corner. Quite a comedown after their outdoor concerts and parties, the "festivals of the oppressed." I was asleep when they were brought here, but the smell of blood woke me up. Then Baron Haussmann arrived, and at first he wouldn't simply lie there and behave himself like a dignified corpse—he tried to reorganize the tombs. We had to sit on him and roll some rocks over to keep him in his place. La Fontaine's grave is visited at night by animals—rumor has it they make pilgrimages from all over France, even Italy. Sarah Bernhardt, so accustomed to adulation herself, is terribly jealous of all the attention Jim Morrison commands. Her tantrums crack the dirt around her tombstone and even wake the living in the *quartier*. No wonder she slept in a coffin while alive. She was sure of eternal applause. As for Jim, I know that he was a seraph out of his element, never meant to be long for this world, and his death had nothing to do with sex, drugs, and rock 'n' roll: it was just time for him to go home. You could tell by looking at his scapulae that he was not really human, that his anatomy included wings, and finally he took flight. And speaking of angels, they blame vandals for breaking off the fingers of Chopin's angel, the lovely one watching over his tomb, but I'll share this last secret with you before I shut up and make my departure: she *chews* her fingernails whenever, throughout the city of Paris, anyone plays Chopin's compositions badly—wrong tempo, wrong notes, out-of-tune piano: she won't tolerate the slightest imper- fection when it comes to his art. And now I'll be on my way, via Le Métro Nécro, of course. I'm off to the Hôtel Jasmin. I heard via our underground radio that a group of sweet young necrophiliacs is arriv- ing there tomorrow, and having been roused from my slumbers, I'm in the mood for a bit of fun.

—*Comtesse Marie de la Rochephoquecriard*

L'EGLISE DES MARIONETTES

"I had imagined that Paris would be grand, glittering, exquisite. I was fearfully disappointed. It looked bleak, dirty, sullen. But then suddenly, as I dutifully puffed at my bitter cigarette, a change crept over the city. A fog had suddenly lifted. The air grew lucid, eloquent. Even the black filtered coffee in the hexagonal brown cups took on a new depth and an insinuating opulence."

—Frederic Prokosch

We include this as a curiosity, not because it's yours to see: the Eglise des Marionettes is one of the most secret sacred places in all of France or even Europe. We know of this church by hearsay and through one garrulous, indiscreet, drunk marionette that *hasard,* chance, threw in our path (literally! the poor little fellow looked a heap of cracked wooden bones and chipped paint, his outfit all awry, and we took him to a quiet square where a fountain helped restore his life and our credulity with the same splashed waters).

The Eglise des Marionettes is by no means a spectacle (don't you think they have enough of that, on a stage that's also a cage?), but a private place of worship for Paris's marionette population and the occasional foreign visitor coming through on tour—mostly rowdy Italians and Dubliners on a spree.

The mass, Eucharist, genuflection are all in mute miniature (so we're told), and confession is an elaborate process expressed entirely through the stylized gestures of which the parish is capable. Our source, a genetic throwback to the days when marionettes could talk, told us how one Sunday morning a priest went missing or broken and they had to grab the first substitute at hand—a strapping minotaur. Apparently, Catholic marionettes can give their masters and manipulators the slip for mass, confession, and an occasional *bouffe* at a small café.

With its congregation of one, this was the address Erik Satie often used as his own when sending letters of friendship, thanks, collaboration. Satie also wrote, addressed, and mailed letters to himself to mark every significant event in his life. The church, quite present and animated without an edifice, called for special notepaper, handwriting, and even manner of dress. The Metropolitan Church of the Art of Jesus Christ the Conductor continues to exist, precisely where it counts, in our imaginations, and in the glow of memory that smiles on in its founder and composer, Erik Satie.

L'EGLISE METROPOLI-TAINE D'ART DE JESUS CONDUCTEUR
THE METROPOLITAN CHURCH OF THE ART OF JESUS CHRIST THE CONDUCTOR

This intimate church, really just a chapel, in the fourteenth *arrondissement* offers regular mass for its parishioners and also attracts an unusual number of nubile girls and lone women. It's common knowledge that the confessors here show no mercy for rapists who wish to cleanse their consciences: they're likely to find themselves in blindfolds on the Eurydice Express (see Transportation, *Buses*). Unlike Sainte Geneviève, who saved Paris from the Huns, or Cornwall's Saint Columba, the fifteen-year-old who saved her village from a bear, Sainte Jacquéline is distinguished by the singularity of her miniature savior. A well-endowed and well-betrothed teenager (the families both rejoicing in the alliance which

PETITE EGLISE DE SAINTE JACQUELINE DU SALAMANDRE
LITTLE CHURCH OF SAINT JACQUELINE OF THE SALAMANDER
38, rue des Trois Capitaines

would combine great masses of land, pigs, cows, and streams), Jacquéline Douxval was bathing in a pond just like the one Monet was to dabble in several centuries later when a passing nobleman leapt from his horse and dragged her out of the water. Imagine his surprise when, about to force his way into the milky young virgin, he came upon a salamander plastered across the very region he was so intent on entering. Nothing he might do could pry the tenacious creature from Jacquéline's pride and shame (good thing for both that his dagger was being sharpened at the blacksmith's that day: he was on his way to collect it), and so young Jacquéline's virtue went unassailed. After this minor miracle, it was decreed and agreed by those who had any say in the matter (the local church hierarchy and Jacquéline's parents) that she should enter a convent and consecrate her so originally preserved purity to the love of her Lord. The salamander decided against vows of chastity for himself, that he might enter the convent with her, and his progeny tend her when his short life had run its course. It must be admitted that the salamander had been a devotee of Our Lady from long before Jacquéline's fateful dip, with his own shrine constructed of willow twigs, rushes, and flowers in season, as well as medallions and crucifixes that other careless passersby and bathers had lost at the edge of his pond.

VILLE DE PARIS

LOST AND FOUND/PERDU ET TROUVE
Français au verso

Please fill out the following form with a description of the lost article(s).

Description: One tour group consisting of approximately 16 people including the tour guide and a straggler who didn't sign up or pay. Most of the people in the group are older and several are wearing matching blue sun caps. All of us were wearing T-shirts that said, "I was a *vedette* on the Pont Neuf." The tour guide is a middle-aged woman (I prefer the French for this: "Une femme d'un certain âge," being one myself), who is of German descent and who admitted freely that she'd been given us by accident as her command of English is really quite haphazard. But what she doesn't know in vocabulary she makes up in volume, which is why I am truly astonished to have misplaced this particular group.

Approximate Location of Lost Object: The crème brûlée shop in the rue Mouffetard.

Approximate Time and Date Object Lost: Today, for heaven's sake! I want to find these clots and clotesses and get my money's worth. Oh, yes, and my husband, too.

Name and Address of Claimant: Ziggie Spurthrast, Rm. #11, Hôtel Carrington.

LE VIOLEUR EN SMOKING

"There are days when everything about us is lucent and ethereal . . . and everything suggestive of spaciousness: the river, the bridges, the long streets, and the lavish squares—has put that spaciousness behind itself, is painted on it as on a tissue of silk."

—Rainer Maria Rilke

Phantom lexicon:

un revenant: ghost
Literally, coming back, coming again
Histoire or *conte de revenants:* ghost story
Ville de revenants: Paris in August

The twentieth arrondissement (*le vingtième, comme on dit*) is a mostly well-behaved *quartier,* and that's not only so because many in it are dead (the Père Lachaise cemetery is here, generally tranquil except for the strange duet in 1980 that resulted from Chopin's and Jim Morrison's only attempt at musical conversation). Somewhat suspended and with the cleanest air in the city, the vingtième has attracted many hospitals, as well as a walkway street named for the writer Villiers de l'Isle Adam.

In the midst of all this decorum, a custom in fits and starts breaks the placid surface at any time, night or day, throughout the year, and grandmothers, mothers, teenagers, even some precocious children pin corsages to their collars, shoulder straps, breasts, lapels to mourn the disappearance, and honor the visiting ghost and memory, of "le violeur en smoking," or The Tuxedo Rapist, as he was referred to in the *International Herald Tribune.* Although he did not confine his assaults to one street, alley, or *trottoir,* he began his career in the Passage des Soupirs, or the Passage of Sighs. Was he a harmless dandy, as the corsages seem to say? All the dapper attacker did, after all, was accost lone women in deserted dark streets and force them to ballroom dance with him. As a signature, he always left a corsage pinned to his victim's heaving bosom, and he spit-shined his own spiffy shoes. So if you are walking uphill from place Gambetta and you see a skirt swishing in 3/4 time, or notice half a tangoed couple about-facing with flashing eyes, you will know that the *phantom en smoking* has reappeared, invisible but much adored.

There are not really any circumstances to be seen here, except the ones you bring with you or improvise under watchful eyes, but Monsieur Robert Reaudrigeau, otherwise a *fabricateur* of fountains who started out life at one of the philosophical preschools of the Sixth Empire, could not simply fill several rooms with a bunch of old clocks he'd collected since passing his baccalaureate the third time around. It is worth buying the pamphlet on sale (updated every year or so) that describes experiences people claim to have had while admiring the circumstances at hand. "Which hand?" you may well wonder, regarding a nearby *grandpère* clock's with suspicion while interrogating your own with a missing glove.

Like the Musée de Gastronomie, Le Musée des Horloges et Circonstances often collaborates with other museums in staging its shows. With the Museum of Detective, or Mystery, Novels (Le Musée des Romans Policiers), it once devoted its rooms (in some cases clocks were stopped or otherwise made to misbehave) to cases of circumstantial evidence, re-creating scenes from Sherlock

MUSEE DES HORLOGES ET CIRCONSTANCES
5, rue des Horloges

"Each room has its own climate. In Claude Monet's room there is a river air.
Looking at Renoir's water you feel blisters on your palm as though you'd been rowing.
Signac invented the maize sun.
The woman who lectures about the pictures leads the cultural workers behind her.
To look at them you'd say a magnet was attracting a duck."

—Osip Mandelstam

Holmes, Agatha Christie, Inspector Maigret. Inspector Clouseau was a tricky one to deal with, all that Pink Panther farce and slapstick, so they did a multimedia presentation and finally simply turned one room into a small cinéma and showed splices of the old movies.

"When Madame des Ricochets rings
The doors burst open to make way for the servants upon
* their see-saws, sliding-ponds, and swings."*
—*André Breton*

MUSEE DE LA PORTE
MUSEUM OF THE DOOR
48, rue Tarneval

[647]The *salon de thé* was the site of a performance art piece, "The Spirits Are Knocking," which was initiated by the spirits themselves, beginning with the invitations sent to selected rooms at the museum's favorite hotels. The guests summoned, the spirits proceeded with a straightforward séance, except that the tables were turned, and then the doorknobs, and then the spirits exchanged places with the living forevermore.

The entrance to this museum takes a while to pass through, and you have many ways to go about it, as from the street you are confronted with twelve doors side by side, and making a choice there is but the beginning, for behind each door is a series of twelve more, and you need not persist in the same line as the one with which you began. Each door has a tale to tell, yours for the asking when you buy the museum's catalogue—a collection of poems, myths, history, short stories, and contemporary confections on the art of getting into or out of a room. The computer installed in 1991 keeps track of visitors and limits their number to avoid stampedes. But we are keeping you from the main room, where the exhibit changes every few months and features works from present-day artists as well as

doors from houses of the famous, the beloved, the
disowned. The side walls have doors leading to a
book and gift shop, a *salon de thé*,[642] and *les toilettes*,
whose doors pose yet further problems for the
unagile and desperate, while the *pièce de résistance*
of the back wall is a series of three revolving
doors leading into the Musée des Spinning Tops.

Yes, the name is awkward, but the last part had
to be added because people kept showing up
with roaring appetites and several guards were
even bitten. Known familiarly as Le Museau de la
Grandiose Bouffe (The Muzzle of the Grandiose
Grub), this beautiful but small museum is dedicated to the arts of eating.

As the French are unashamed to admit how
consummately food permeates every aspect of
life, Le Musée de Gastronomie frequently creates
collections with other museums. Pâtés and foie
gras alone have been featured in a number of
such collections, including *Pâté de Soie Raw* and
Pâté Coussin-Coussine—*Pâté of Raw Silk* and *Pâté
Cushion-Cushion*, playing on the film about two
cousins—an exhibit mounted in collaboration
with Le Musée des Arts Décoratifs. A detective
novel exhibit featured *Pâté Belle-Mère* (based on
one of Simenon's more gruesome mysteries about
a murdered mother-in-law)—in a collection
assembled with Le Musée des Romans Policiers.

**MUSEE DE
GASTRONOMIE MAIS
PAS DEGUSTATION**
THE MUSEUM OF
GASTRONOMY BUT
NOT TASTING
**456, rue Antonin
Carême**

A small wax museum in the
cellar portrays such famous
gastronomes as Brillat-
Savarin, Alexandre Dumas,
Carême, Escoffier, MFK
Fisher (lately acknowledged
by the French for her *savoir-
vivre* and her impeccable
prose), Rabelais, and Julia
Child.

⁂ "In Paris in 1911, the first cubist baby was born to an unwed mother from Avignon. She gave birth to him on the plaza in front of the tan buildings of the Louvre under a typically gray Paris sky. She was a large angular woman, the planes of her thighs, pelvis, and breasts meeting sharply. She made no sound as she lay flat against the gray ground. Picking up her child—not the squalling, squirming thing that most newborns are but rather stiff and pale— she had trouble holding on to his amorphous body that took on the colors of his birthplace. She felt, as she walked away, that his many-angled body fit easily against her own and then again, that he grew or shrank and, suddenly, that her baby had far too many elbows."

—Maya Sonenberg

Naturally, Agatha Christie's Hercule Poirot was also featured in the *salle des gratinées,* his name in sound so very close to *poireau,* that is, leek. An array of music-based pâtés included "Pâté de Ma Mère Oye," Saint-Saëns's little *chef d'oeuvre* and *hors d'oeuvre* Mother Goose Suite playing in the background—here the collaboration was with Radio Courtoisie.

Since appetites are whipped into quite a froth by this viewing (provided you don't ponder the *Pâté Belle-Mère* too long), the neighborhood positively swarms your senses with a festive selection of restaurants and *espaces de dégustation,* tasting rooms, where you really can try the day's inventions, the past's enduring classics, tomorrow's *plat-sibilités du jour.*

Of particular interest for the vistor without much time is the Salle d'Entrées, whose entry fee is at *tarif reduit,* reduced fee. Many like to drop in here on the way to a dinner engagement as a bit of foreplay before the rest of the fun begins. That's one reason a location so susceptible to various métro lines (Numbers 3, 5, 6, 8, 10 all run shudderingly close to the wax museum of *grands bouffeurs*) was selected when the *Ministre de Goût* (Minister of Taste) was chewing over the various possibilities on an edible Plan de Paris created by Fauchon for the deliberations and of course the publicity such a Paris à la Carte was sure to generate. So, it's Métro Mange. Don't take yourself to

Métro Monge in the fifth by mistake, although if you do, Les Délices d'Aphrodite will more than placate you in ambience as well as *bouffe:* Greek raised to the nearly sublime.

LES DELICES D'APHRODITE

When you enter, your ticket is a kiss on the wrist, lipstick varying with which cosmetics company has paid how much to so advertise its colored mouths. Le Musée des Lèvres et Livres is an intimate experience, so don't come here unless you are prepared to leave your armor at the *vestiaire* and, when applicable, promenade your *amour* through its rooms. The lips by Man Ray greet you without saying a word, although they are blown up to fifty times their original size.

The museum's permanent collection includes handmade books, first editions, paintings in which lips figure prominently or whose lips are especially luscious (be sure to twinkle your eyes at Gabriel Nalou's miniature of *Mademoiselle Henriette Lacépède Donnant une Bise à sa Levrette—Mademoiselle Henriette Lacépède Giving Her Greyhound a Smooch*—and David's great unknown, unsung *Quatre Lèvres au Bord d'une Bataille—Four Lips at the Edge of a Battle*); paintings that portray the act of reading, or anything else going on in the presence or proximity of books (Fantin-Latour's paintings of his sisters gently inclining their faces over books are always

MUSEE DES LEVRES ET LIVRES
MUSEUM OF LIPS AND BOOKS
39, bd Brume

WORDS TO MOUTH:
🗣️I'd like to buy this book, but there's a mouth holding it shut.
✳️*J'aimerais acheter ce livre mais il y a une bouche qui le tient fermé.*

🗣️Ah, very well—there's a dentist on call at my hotel.
✳️*Ah, tant mieux—il y a un dentiste à la demande à mon hôtel.*

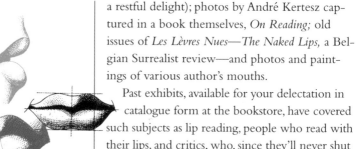

a restful delight); photos by André Kertesz cap-
tured in a book themselves, *On Reading;* old
issues of *Les Lèvres Nues—The Naked Lips,* a Belgian Surrealist review—and photos and paintings of various author's mouths.

Past exhibits, available for your delectation in
catalogue form at the bookstore, have covered
such subjects as lip reading, people who read with
their lips, and critics, who, since they'll never shut
up, have been installed in their own rooms, some
in person—these can be very vexing or tedious.
You can also retire to a pleasant café in the
museum's courtyard and try their *tarte trois mous-
quetaires, salade frisée aux museaux de porc* (it's not
only the endive that is *frisée* here: the pigs' muzzles
are also dried and shredded very fine, so you wind
up eating curled lips—a shiver for Elvis, if you
please), and a *crème brûlée* that is still burning, so it
gives your lips something to think about while
the aesthetic experience you've just been having
goes on reading your mind.

MUSEE DU CINEMA
CINEMA MUSEUM
HENRI LANGLOIS

At the Montparnasse Cemetery you can lay cel-
luloid flowers on the grave of Henri Langlois.
His grave is literally one of the most picturesque
in all of Paris, as the tombstone is covered with
very fine photos of decades of movie stars.
Langlois founded and sustained out of his own
love and pockets the Musée du Cinéma and the

Cinémathèque, and he was joined by Lotte Eisner, who'd hidden the classic German films from the Nazis and eventually brought them to Paris. It's one of these German Expressionist films that a pair of rolling eyes demands we watch here. *The Golem* was made in 1914 by supernatural director Paul Wegener, who, clad from head to foot in clay-caked cloth, also played the title character, a creature fabricated by a rabbi in Prague to help his people, being persecuted by an evil emperor. The museum's fabulous collection of film sets, costumes, and memorabilia includes the figure of the Golem, kept in a glass case, with his Dutch-boy haircut, huge, encumbered body, and the star on his chest.[16]

It's never been easy to figure out Le Musée du Cinéma, its odd hours, its insistence on visitors prowling only with a guide, but these are minor quirks compared to the events of 1988–89, when the staff started showing up sporadically, faking illnesses at Le Malade Imaginaire pharmacies all over town, and staging supernatural strikes—supernatural in origin. All claimed that the Golem was rolling his eyes at them, even fidgeting with the amulet on his breast, the very thing to set him in motion, on a rampage, that is. Staff who didn't quit were fired, only to be replaced with others, soon terrified. And then these fears took their first big clumsy steps, for the Golem, so attuned to his own city, felt his

From the cinéma at the Montparnasse Cemetery

[16] further details await you in Prague!

"The Place Dauphine is certainly one of the most profoundly secluded places I know of, one of the worst wastelands in Paris. Whenever I happen to be there, I feel the desire to go somewhere else gradually ebbing out of me, I have to struggle against myself to get free from a gentle, over-insistent, and, finally, crushing embrace."

—André Breton

analog of a heart beat beneath his amulet at the very hour that the keys were jingling in Wenceslas Square. His eyes popping, he broke out of his case, then the Palais de Chaillot, and lumbered his way to the Marais, the old Jewish ghetto of Paris, knocking down high-tech *salons de thé*, bric-a-brac boutiques, and all the other products of gentrification that have changed the Marais in the last decades. He did stop off at Goldenberg's for some blintzes and picnic supplies to sustain him during his long journey through Mittleuropa—and headed east, straight for the Magic Lantern Theatre Velvet Revolution.

"I fell in love with Paris, not ecstatically, as later on, but with suspicion and uneasiness, as though expecting to be betrayed. What did it was the sunlight as it flowed over the buildings, with the reticence and spellbound absorption of a dream. I leaned over the parapet of the Pont du Carrousel and watched the shadows crawling along the opposite shore. The towers of Notre Dame grew incandescent, like lanterns. Or I paused in an alley near the Place du Tertre and saw the flash of sunset on the domes of Sacré-Coeur, transforming it into a mosque in the middle of a desert. The city was transfigured by this play of light and shadow into a maze of human wonder, human sorrow, and human wickedness."

—*Frederic Prokosch*

PLACE DAUPHINE

"Just in front of my home, Christo, the exterior decorator, put a skirt around the Pont Neuf. I always said that Paris is a woman, I mean, female. In fact, the sex of Paris is just there, behind the waist of Pont Neuf: place Dauphine. You may know this lovely triangle-shaped place, covered with *accueillants* nice trees.

"By the way, you might be interested knowing that a few years ago, some people from the 'National Historical Monuments' X-rayed the huge statue of our beloved and juicy King Henry IV (he was the one who said, 'Chaque dimanche, une poule au pot pour chacun'; at that time there wasn't fast food and Love Burger; frenchmen were eating lentil soup if lucky). The purpose of this expensive manipulation was to check on eventual cracks in the statue. The surprise was BIG. Inside this statue is another statue, smaller and which represents Napoleon. I can hear you from here: 'How is it possible that a statue of King Henry the IV is pregnant with a statue of Emperor Napoleon who was himself not yet conceived in History?!' I have the answer: the original statue of Henry was melted during the French Revolution, probably to make cannons, and it's only in 1818 that a replica was cast with the bronze from a Napoleon statue. The fondeur, a fervent Bonapartiste, enclosed a small statue of his hero in the big one.

"You have to admit that I am lucky. I live so close to the sex of Paris that it's a perpetual incest. I am sunk in it."

—Jean-Jacques Passera

*P*aris is a completely clothed city. With the brutal winds slashing off the Seine, this is exigent. I have not once seen a nude stalking the streets; they are all in the museums, eating on the grass, although I did see a topless *clocharde* on a métro bench the other day mending her sweaters and socks. Rearriving in Paris after ten weeks' absence in London, I felt the change acutely: Parisians I'd last seen in August were at once camouflaged and exposed by their winter clothes. Strangers in the street and friends startled me with their new found beauty, as if they were animals who had grown hibernal fur, thickly coated and repossessingly booted, wrapped in scarves of angora, silk, spangles— rectangles or squares.

I hypothesize the winter-augmented disgruntlement in the métro to be suffocation by sheep. The wool spreads through the métro car a kind of sullen torpor over legs of corduroy. Everyone is so well defended it's terrifying when they have to touch. Through women's coats and scarves run streaks of gold that catch a light not really in their eyes or hair, but may throw off some internal flame.

I am the object of blatant curiosity in my two pairs of *chaussettes* (socks) stuffed into a pair of sandals. I think of the painting by Magritte of the shoes that are at the same time feet, toes protruding out of leather soles, toenails that are nearly eyes. I go to find the post-card of them at Beaubourg but they have disappeared, having walked away, I conjecture, toward Morocco, the land of tangerines.

On a rare afternoon of immense sunlight pouring through a frag-ile February sky, I go to the Grand Palais to see the paintings of

Claude Gellé (the frozen one) le Lorrain, and what hits me as I walk into the first *grande salle* is the vision of all these black-coated forms moving against the eternal spring and summer he painted: apricot dawns, blues and greens, inhumanly pink human flesh.

When I go to La Tartine for a coffee and tartine on *pain Poilane,* in removing my coat as I advance toward a table (all of them seem to be in corners even though the room has only the usual number of corners, and many more tables than that) or arrive at it, flinging my arms free and crawling out of its weight, I feel as if I am divesting myself of a bear. "It's my bear," "C'est mon ourse," I explain as I look for some place to stash it: it takes up a whole chair by itself and may be hungry for all I know. It feeds on my body, stealing my warmth to give it back to me, and what's more it's reversible and Chinese, but it's *not* a panda bear.

. . . *La Mode* is *le monde,* the world, feminized and with the *n* removed. What did that *n* stand for before they took it away? Nudity? Nothingness? The No between the body and the soul?

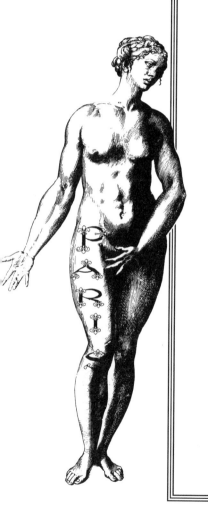

In the days of hats, and it's sad they're
seriously over, a hat was a catastrophe
if it failed to provoke a witticism from
some man in the street. La Mode was
the muse prowling the pavement,
evoking poems from anyone at all.

. . . I go for a swim at La Piscine
Pontoise. To get there I cross three
bridges. When I arrive I undress and
clothe myself for the water, a strange
custom but that's how it is. Back in my
room I feel something watching me as
I slip into my nightgown, diaphanous
collaboration with nudity and a
reprieve from Levi Strauss. Among the
books lying on my bed a small glass
button reposes, the eye that must have
followed me home, for it does not
belong to anything in my closet, and
it's never seen me before. I enter the
eye and see the closets of Paris spilling
out into the boulevards.

STORES *and* SHOPPING

"... every one of its show windows is an erogenous zone that the tongue of a look caresses ... we'll look at them, yes, knowing them to be a living part of a total tremor, of an intimacy to which we finally have access. ... the city that has the most shop windows in the world and the most looks in the world caressing the windows. Licking them, the city says."

—Julio Cortázar

O PTI CIEN. Jean Gérôme. Enseigne murale—Peinture avec cadre à attributs. 1902. From Concours d'enseignes de la Ville de Paris 1902. Bibliothèque Nationale, Paris.

Unlike the other *grands magasins,* department stores, such as La Samaritaine, Galeries Lafayette, and Printemps, where everything is under one roof, or several adjacent roofs, Grand Magasin Molière is found throughout the city as a collection of individual shops, all named after plays by Molière. Tartuffe, or the Impostor, for instance, is always a front for something else, whatever it purports to be selling, and is just down rue de la Faisanderie from the Counterfeit Museum. The Bourgeois Gentleman is in the posh sixteenth arrondissement, halfway between Balzac's pavilion and Monet's Musée Marmottan. The Imaginary Invalid, of course, is everywhere, a pharmacy to take care of both real and faked maladies. The pharmacists are more perceptive than most doctors and know whether medication is called for or if a cuddle in the back room will do (they prefer this to placebos). One nice touch to the Imaginary Invalid alludes to Molière's noble gesture on the eve of his death: gravely (and truly) ill, he insisted on playing the title role despite protests of his company and loved ones. "It's hard to die," he said, but at the suggestion of cancelling the performances, he replied, "How can I deprive fifty workmen of their bread?" Thus each Imaginary Invalid opens next to a *boulangerie.*

The Misanthrope, whose merchandise is of no importance, started out near La Comédie

GRAND MAGASIN MOLIERE

Grands Magasins Molière namesake. After Mignard.

Essential vocabulary at The Imaginary Invalid:

chercher: Search.

As when one enters a pharmacie: *"Vous cherchez, Madame?"* or *"Vous désirez, Madame?"* or *"Qu'est-ce qu'il vous faut?"* You can respond: *"Oui, je cherche l'élixir de la jeunesse perpétuelle"* or *"Je cherche le secret de la vie éternelle."*

"Psychology, that old freak, whose presence at the hairdresser's is scarcely noticeable apart from the names of perfumes, the idea of hair dyes, and the romanticism of the various hairstyles . . . no longer holds any secrets for tailors, and hasn't done for a long time. For example, right at the end of the Galerie du Thermomètre we find Vodable who attracts customers by calling himself: *Fashionable Tailor*. He also sells trunks, and, as he puts it in his careful English, *All Travelling Requisities*. I can't help feeling that that sensitive experimenter Landru must have bought his clothes here, trying on suits in the middle of luggage displayed like so many mysterious symbols of his destiny."

—Louis Aragon

Française, giving work to struggling young actors plus a chance to sharpen their tongues in repartée and scurrilous phrases. Half the customers, however, were not tender-witted theater-goers but highly experienced actors, for whom the young puppies were no match, so the shop was moved to St-Germain-des-Prés, to liven the smug place up and offer a diversion from the showcase cafés and cinémas. A lesser-known play, *The Flying Doctor,* has tendered its namesake's ministrations to pilots of The Fur's Going to Fly and rounded up, by tagging along with them, students for The School for Wives. The Miser did not last long as a *bureau de change,* money exchange, since its rates were so unfavorable for every currency and tourist that most customers walked away broke, and the word soon got around.

Food lovers should not miss the Charcuterie Monsieur de Pourceaugnac, which translates roughly "gentleman from Pig Province" and sells not only ham and sausages but also regional products from the Limousin, like Molière's poor protagonist, whom Paris abused through farce. But how appropriately! A sausage is stuffed, and so is the drama form, which is how it got that name— *farce* = stuffing. A snatch of song from *Monsieur de Pourceaugnac*'s masquerade ball is suspended above the salamis and sausages: "When we gather for the sake of laughter,/The wisest people, it seems to me,/Are those who are most mad."

This shop in Montparnasse, conveniently located near the cemetery where lie the dead poets resurrected on their pants, sells *pantalons* for both major sexes in fabrics of *velour* (velvet), *coton, corde du roi* (corduroy), *soie* (silk) both *crue et raffinée* (raw and refined)—to name a few. Special items may be ordered in such materials as *carton* (cardboard) to commemorate Dada's first historical night in Zurich; and vellum for medieval religious verse or love songs of the troubadours (the latter with option of supplementary lady's girdle if the customer to be panted is a true knight at heart); and any fabric you might bring with you for a custom-tailored purchase, *sur mesure* (not *fur mesure,* although fur pants are grown on the premises if an exceptionally Baltic winter is in store).

Le but—the aim—of this enterprise is to spread poetry across Paris by the seat of one's pants, whether trotting it about on the *trottoirs* or sitting on it along the *quais, métro, banquettes.* In this fashion, Parisians and tourists express their passions, hopes, beliefs—through the words of Villon, Lousabine, Valéry, Mallarmé, Boris Vian, Jacques Roubaud, and their illustrious *copains* et *copines.* When the shop first opened, *derrières* were rife with Neruda, Akhmatova, Unomuno, Vachu, Bukowski, Basho, but pressure from the Académie Française and the Ministère de Culture swiftly obliged the shop to tailor its trade

ARSE POETICA
39, rue des
Marmonniers

"Très hip!" says Alec Bloc in *Le Point Tordu.*

To give you an idea of what's possible, we offer a few orders that were actually placed and then put in their place. A pair of white velvet smoking trousers walked off with these words of Max Jacob:
"What a winter that one of 1929 was! Paris in white velvet, all the windows like moonstones."

A bellhop took the bold step of self-expression by having one of the *152 Proverbs Adapted to the Taste of the Day* by Paul Eluard and Benjamin Péret stitched onto his uniform:
"To seize the blond man by his luggage."

An original from customer
Alf Musket, of Austin, Texas:
"Still the perfume comes
    from your shadow,
sweet little tumbleweed gal
    of mine."

And a sampling off other
unnamed haunches:
"Between your legs, quick
    with flames,
the narrow muzzle of a fox."
    —Claude Royet-Journoud

A different pair of velvet
pants for a customer with a
darker vision bears these
lines from Louis Aragon:
"Evening soars down with
    silent wingbeats, joining
A velvet Breughel to this
    Breughel of hell."

along the lines of the great classics and contemporaries of France. Nevertheless, some of her favorite adopted daughters and sons have met with official approval; if you're game, just give them a try.

Naturellement, two walls are lined with volumes of poetry, and the shop, so backside-friendly, provides an array of chairs and divans to assure that one's choice can be arrived at *en tout confort,* in all comfort. Besides collected works and anthologies, hefty bound volumes of stanzas and sonnets, quatrains and villanelles are yours to leaf through for purposes of commerce and the meaning of life, but you'll be greeted most graciously if you arrive with poem in hand. Americans, with their overall larger buttocks, can handle *grosser mots,* vulgar, but with adipose, words and meatier swatches of verse.

If you have any afterthoughts, you can tuck them into the special back pocket for these (and for little books)—on an embroidered handkerchief softly declaiming your message. These must be bought by the *dixaine,* ten, each with a different and original phrase, and are exclusively available to your specifications at Motchoir, on rue des Larmes et Lions.

SHAKESPEARE & CO
37, rue de la Bûcherie

I was sitting in Shakespeare and Company, reading Kafka's diary, and copying out an entry about a whip I know too well ("We are permitted to crack that whip, the will, over us with our own hand"), then sensed (a mild lashing) it was time to go, so I stood up and walked over to Laurel hovering over a table of books, and as I arrived there, wine began to pour out of the ceiling onto my head, splashing onto my right foot, and onto my purse. Something was definitely happening on the floor above, the one you reach by crawling up a red ladder with Yeats's "foul rag-and-bone shop of the heart" quote pointing the way. I had been writing, earlier that day while sitting on some steps near place de la République, a tiny letter to Michael in London, and the wine seeping into my purse marked the very pages in my *carnet* I was writing to him. Wine stain became a historical marker of itself, the story materialized on the page.

A *folie à deux* is a madness for two, the kind you wish would last, but Folios à Deux is a bookstore that takes twosome at its word. There will always be two copies of a given book, many books are bilingual, and you must buy two books or none at all. This stipulation is good for business if you only wanted one, and that one badly enough you'll gladly grab something else,

FOLIOS A DEUX
77, rue des Anciens Calomnies

but the choreography gets a bit complicated when you've selected a stack of titles and have to go through the line at the cashier's again and again. Most people, therefore, come in pairs or gangs, and speaking of pairs, Folios à Deux does specialize in books that take on new meanings when read together, one of the endangered if not lost arts of love.

LE GRENIER DE TANTE AMELIE
13, galerie des Corbeaux

Le grenier, the attic, of Tante Amélie has long ago been exhausted, but when her charming niece Juliette got into her basement—*quelle trouvaille!*— what a find! Buttons, baseball cards, tonsils, teeth, old sweethearts you left on the shelf—anything you've ever lost or misplaced could have found its way into Amélie's *sous-sol* (basement). The Bureau of Missing Persons even turned up several Jim Morrison fans here who'd disappeared on separate excursions to his grave. Incongruously, they were all chained to a television set that once belonged to Marlene Dietrich (not for sale: Tante Amélie and Dietrich used to smoke together on boulevard des Italiens). In spite of this one incident, there is no connection whatsoever between Tante Amélie's and Le Service Kidnapping.

Juliette knows how much these reacquaintances with lost items can mean to the bereft, so the prices are a bit steep, as are the stairs she

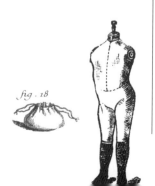

fig . 18

moved into the attic to dislocate the basement, just for atmosphere.

A word of advice: Juliette, a keen observer, will be looking for traces of recognition flickering across your face (betraying your emotions could drastically raise the price), so it's a good idea to spend a few nights with a *jeu de cartes,* card game, preferably poker, at Aux Déboires de Petrouchka, which keeps a few tables reserved for this purpose, in honor of one of Stravinsky's vices and his ballet score *Jeu de Cartes.*

Clear across town from Arse Poetica, near place Gambetta, is a straightforward *pantalon* pavilion with no axiom to grind. Pantalone features a veritable Columbine *à la caisse,* taking your cash, and offers a wide array of pants for men in the prime of their life. Here you will find Penitential Pants, fresh out of the oven *Paintalons,* Presto Pants (one swift kick and they're off), and for the big guys (*les gars gros ou costauds*) Pantagruel and Pavarotti pants. On slow days, *pantrons* will be invited into an alcove with displays and albums and videos showing pants through the ages—quite an eye-opener when you consider that it's only through the last few centuries of the western world that men have encased themselves in these things.

Still, if they must do it, Pantalone provides variety, and can also run up a suit in collabora-

PANTALONE
65, rue des Zouaves

Zouave

Au fur et à mesure is not a phrase that will come in handy at Pantalone. It means: gradually as it goes along.

tion with the *Jacketier* (dreadful anglicism surely on its last legs) facing you as you cross the pleasant place Gambetta. Métro Gallieni.

BASKET
49, rue Madame

Named after Gertrude Stein's big white poodles Basket (in succession, not simultaneous), this shop on rue Madame not far from Stein's rue de Fleurus caters to Parisians and tourists who pamper their pets more than themselves and each other. Dogs get the most space and attention here, but a few toys are thrown in for cockatoos, ocelots, and baby ostriches. Boutique Basket comes with an impressive pedigree and endorsements from both a leading veterinarian and restaurateur Simon Aboit of Patte à la Main, who orders the special monogrammed bibs here for his hairy and monosyllabic customers. Bejeweled leashes for bejowled dowagers with pugs; pewter bowls from Nancy; rawhide bones and beef jerky from the American Wild West; bone china from rue de Paradis; brushes of boar bristles from Nîmes, made by Protestant monks; tapestry cushions from Cité des Gobelins; and a fine selection of snacks and treats made from scraps at Fauchon and Gargantua—well, you get the picture, and its bite is as big as its bark, the bite it takes out of your wallet, that is.

Very far away from the wound-up Avanti is the *très très décontracté,* very very relaxed, Ralenti, where your travails are lifted off your shoulders by hands that are strangers to the sorts of hands running around in circles at Le Musée des Horloges et Circonstances. They do this to put you in a receptive attitude toward their clothes from the comfort zone. *Chemises,* shirts, that were born to be rumpled, trousers that do your breathing for you, dressing gowns and party gowns for a party of two, shoes and slippers of supple leather, satin stitched onto soles. Some clothes are unisex, others very much not so, if you have attracting the opposite sex in mind and wish to distinguish yourself. It's pleasant to spend half an hour here with no intention of making a purchase (as long as you pretend a little), to listen to sloweddown, softer speech, feel a light pressure on your instep as you slip into a pair of mules. The only problem with this place is that they have to keep moving, and this keeps the clerks a bit more on edge than was the intention: *ralentir* means to slow down, and as each *quartier* they come to speeds up, they're up and running again themselves.

RALENTI
33, rue des Eventails

TOUS LES DEUX: BRASSERIE et BRASSIERIE
94–96, rue Liliane de Pouvoir

We're still not sure we should be leaving this establishment in Stores or if we'd be better off putting it with Restaurants. Nevertheless, it's here now. Tous les Deux is a brasserie/brassièrie serving beer, choucroute, and Alsatian specialties on the one side and offering various underthings such as brassières on the other side. The owners, a charming married couple, decided to combine their establishments after noticing busloads of Americans stopping in at the Brasserie looking for fancy French knickers and a steady stream of French coming to the Brassièrie searching for refreshment. Highlights include the fashion shows presented at lunch hour and the snack bar service for customers using the changing rooms.

LA TOUCHERIE
5, place des Papillons

Libre service, self-service, is starting to be touted at some of the small neighborhood *épiceries,* grocery shops, and is permitted in the occasional *supermarché,* supermarket, but the prevailing sentiment among *primeurs* (those who sell fruit and vegetables in shops or at open-market stalls) is HANDS OFF, and you'll just have to hope they find you charming or deserving as they decide which apples and pears, carrots and green beans to sell you. They won't be the ones you'd choose. You'll find through experience who will respond to your discernment or pleading eyes. Tunisians tend to be friendlier about this. If you indicate

continued on page 142

"MY CORSET MAKER"

". . . she says to me, 'I don't want my hips anymore! Do something!' So, I lengthen her corsets with a yank, and I tighten them at the bottom, hah! . . . Little by little the fat moves, descending down the thigh. But it was making a roll on the thigh. I lengthen the corset again with a yank and tighten, hah . . . So that Madame P. ended up having her rolls of fat way low, down where it can barely be seen. . . . It's the same for the bust."

"Well, you grab hold of the breast, like this . . . Don't be afraid! I'll explain it to you with a bit of cloth. You grab hold of the breast, here, like this, and fold it, at the bottom, as you press it back as far as you can on the sides. Over that, you put a little brassiere: my 14A, gorgeous! Strictly speaking, it's not a brassiere, it's a small piece of elastic fabric for keeping the breast in position. And over all that, you put my corset, my large 327, the wonder of the day. And there you are, with a divine silhouette; no more hips, stomach, or rear than a bottle of Rhine wine, and especially, the chest of a youth. Having the chest of a youth, that's what matters. But it took some doing to get it that way. Well, Madame, I have competitors who've invented a lot of little things: a stretch fabric, an elastic band to compress and tighten the two halves of the rear end, the crotch clasp, but I can say that I was the first to make practical, and truly aesthetic, the arrangement of the 'folded breast'!"

—*Colette*

that *those* endives, with darkened centers, are corrupted in their very hearts, they might say, "Ah, but you have only to say so: here are the best ones, for you! Just ask me next time." And with service like this, *libre* or not, there really will be a next time.

But let's proceed to the next stage of foreplay (with your goods, that is). *Mademoiselles et Madames,* be warned: M. Bofant is a terrible flirt, but his collection of produce is so sensational that it's no skin off your back to go through the insinuating pleasantries, the personal questions (you can always lie, and change the story next time, since he doesn't remember either answers or faces)—and the touching referred to in his shop's name is between you and the merchandise, not him and his customers.

You pay according to how many individual peppers, endives, apples, cherries, peaches you've touched, added in with the weight of your actual purchases (it's all recorded on video to back up M. Bofant's assistants' tallied observations, so it's best to arrive with sharp vision, a firm sense of purpose, and good eye-hand coordination). You should bear in mind that others will be just as fastidious and won't want to buy the bruises you've left on all this delicate flesh. At least here you get to roll something softly over and see the secret underside that most *primeurs* spend their spare time contriving to hide from you.

TRANSPORTATION

"How tightly packed in we were on that bus platform! And how stupid and ridiculous that young man looked! And what was he doing? Well, if he wasn't actually trying to pick a quarrel with a chap who—so he claimed!—the young fop! kept on pushing him! And then he didn't find anything better to do than to rush off and grab a seat which had become free! Instead of leaving it for a lady!

"Two hours after, guess whom I met in front of the gare Saint-Lazare! The same fancy-pants! Being given some sartorial advice! By a friend!

"You'd never believe it!"

—On the 84 bus with
Raymond Queneau

JOUR
parle aux Français
ET NUIT

QUESTIONS, ANSWERS
USE
Railway Trai
[To buy a ticket, etc., at

URSES
S-NORD
NTILLY
ME CLASSE
ET RETOUR
EMENT POUR
RE CLASSE
5.00

LIQUE · FRANÇA
PUBLIQUE FRANC

ST ARRIVÉ
20 Francs

PASSEPORT

USE ONLY WITH COPPER
BRANCH CIRCUIT CONDUCTORS.
EMPLOYER UNIQUEMENT AVEC
DES CONDUCTEURS DE
DERIVATION EN CUIVRE.

(14)
(15)
(18)
(19)

LE MÉTRO-NÉCRO✝

N° 125   27 Août 1903   40 Cent.

L'Assiette
au Beurre

DESSINS DE
STEINLEN, WIDHOPFF, GALANIS
D'OSTOYA, FLORANE
VAN DONGEN, HRADECKY, POULBOT
CAMARA

Steinlen

Choices for you abound in approaching the métro, bus, and RER lines as you become a veritable passenger. There's the weekly *hebdo,* the monthly *carte orange,* individual tickets (ridiculous), the ten-ticket *carnet.* But the *carte de séjour,* sojourn card, which permits you to stay in the Taupique and Taupinière, could prove invaluable for the truly peripatetic. It extends your options *jusqu'au bout,* to the limits, from the central Taupique to all those RER stations and métro line ends where the Taupinière holds sway: Porte Dauphine, Pont de Levallois, Porte de Clignancourt, Pont de Sèvres, Porte d'Orléans, Porte de la Chapelle, the outskirts of Paris and her suburban crinolines (sorry, but one of the waiters at the Tous les Deux Brasserie et Brassièrie took over this piece, and has underwear on his mind).

At short notice, when these hotels run out of rooms, they simply commandeer a few métro cars and roll out the mattresses (you may not have noticed that the seats are fold-down). But you're likely to wake up in a different station and will not have the benefit of showers at the Taupique or Taupinière, where your night began, since at daybreak the cars join trains again and you're suddenly part of the rush-hour scene: not very picturesque, but a taste of real life *à la Parisienne* —and you haven't even brushed your teeth!

INTRODUCTION

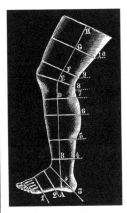

Thoughtfully posted signs indicate distances between major sights.

Watch for this sign indicating that bare feet are permitted!

PARIS A PIED

"How oddly this light
suffuses the covered
arcades which abound in
Paris in the vicinity of the
main boulevards and which
are rather disturbingly
named passages, as though
no one had the right to
linger for more than an
instant in those sunless corridors. A glaucous gleam,
seemingly filtered through
deep water, with the special
quality of pale brilliance of
a leg suddenly revealed
under a lifted skirt."

—Louis Aragon

Many are the ways Paris allows you to caress
and cross her, the most becoming being often
by foot. Gone are the days when Romantic poet
Gerard de Nerval paraded his lobster on a leash,
but you're quite welcome to see how far you can
get with your own lobster or lover by your side.
Although you are perfectly in your rights to walk
where and as you please, you'll have much more
clout in any dispute or *passage* if you walk very
carefully into your local *mairie* (housing the government that administers each arrondissement)
and apply for a *permis de piéton,* pedestrian per-
mit. This document comes in numerous classes,
and if you think it likely you'll be taking bolder
steps one day, it's best to arm your legs with one
of the high-class *permis,* which are attractive and
can be framed to hang on your wall when you
return home to your cabernet sauvignon and
your brie. So here are your principal choices: *piéton provincial (*provincial pedestrian), *piéton privé*
(private pedestrian), *piéton maison* (house, or at-
home pedestrian), *piéton ordinaire* (ordinary
pedestrian), *piéton perdu* (lost pedestrian), *piéton
confondu* (confused pedestrian). The last two are
the most popular with tourists, and allow you to
sit in a special line at any Bureau de Bouleversements you tumble into seeking shelter, succor,
and whereabouts. It's usually the longest line, but
because chairs are part of the treatment, you'll
hardly notice the hours slouching by. *Piéton mai-*

son is a category you might consider if you are subletting an apartment for six months or have otherwise managed to extend your stay that was supposed to be three weeks, for *le p.m.* can sometimes expedite your trip up six flights: rather than wait for the elevator, you may take the stairs. An added feature for the *piéton maison* is a pair of slippers from any of the participating department stores and bazaars, or *souks*. *Piéton provincial* is something of a joke, usually a birthday present from one Parisian to another: an affectionate insult, in short.

Mais passons! The next level includes *piéton sans pitié* (without mercy), which gives you the right to spit on the sidewalk *or* street, and also to stare down a driver as you oblige him to let you cross his path; *piéton politique* (political pedestrian), which grants the citizen no protection during a violent strike, although it carries a certain faded prestige; *piéton pince nez* for the short-sighted (not many pedestrians realize the great value of this one, nor how easy it is to fake the test); *piéton fesses/cuisses* (buttocks/thighs: surely on its way out: incredible the feminists haven't stormed the *mairies*); and, for the senior citizens who take a little longer and have even petitioned for separate lanes of foot traffic so as not to be jostled and knocked over by youngsters in their fifties, *piéton gris* (gray).

Beyond these and a few that delicacy forbids me to mention, there is the *piéton possessif* (for couples); *piéton chaussons rouges* (red shoes); *piéton progressif;* and *piéton pensif* (pensive), for walking lost in one's thoughts. Do not confuse this last option with the *permis de flâneur/flâneuse* (not entirely translatable from one culture to another, but it's something like hanging out, loafing, slouching around, halfway between pose and motion, like a symbolist or existential dandy), which is to be obtained from a different department altogether, and despite its frivolous connotations is not to be taken lightly, as it requires a suitable wardrobe and appropriate presence—or absence—of mind.

METRO JOSEPHINE

While at the Clinique Joséphine be sure to stroke the fertility sculptures by Julio Silva, Satchmo Gandhi, Réhane Ardoise, and Morgana Jouberton in the Graeco-Hindu-Spanish courtyard and to contemplate *all* the lusty images among fauns, flora, fires, and fountains in the pagan temple. The belly dancing here is strictly by women for women, as it was originally intended to be.

METRO MONDRIAN

The only information available at publication date is the following map:

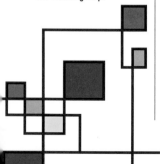

Named for France's two great Joséphines—Napoléon's Empress Joséphine and expatriate American dancer Josephine Baker—this métro station takes the cake for its hybrid décor: the overblown opulence of Empire style with masterpieces of the Harlem Renaissance and assorted Africanalia of the sort that touched off Cubism with Picasso's *Les Demoiselles d'Avignon*. Uninhibited dancing is not only permitted but expected while passengers await their trains, and if you wish to do so with little or no clothing on, the *flics*, cops, will look the other way, after taking a good look, so they can look at someone else.

Should you be coming through this station to visit the district of Floumourtin with its market street full of geese and ganders, hair ribbons and old cancan knickers, cherries from La Vallée des Souverains, and the very assorted cheeses from La Crémerie Biologique Zoovalse, it's worth your while to pop into the maternity and fecundity clinic, Clinique Joséphine, just out the south *sortie*, exit, from Métro Joséphine. It's in mournful homage to the Empress, divorced by Napoléon for having borne him no children, and to Josephine Baker for the tremendous troupe of adopted children she collected and directed.

*E*ntering the métro car, I walk into a Surrealist tableau. Sitting in the midst of all this wool, sweat, and disagreeability, a black woman holds a large rectangular mirror face-up in her ample lap. Faces get caught in it from above as they and it move around. Across the aisle from me, between a pair of knees, grows a large tropical plant. A vacuum cleaner is dragged along like a dog (sign in métro: "Est-ce-que l'idée de perdre votre chien vous affole?"—roughly translated: does the idea of losing your dog flabbergast you?) and gets out at Père Lachaise. Is Oscar Wilde expecting him? Before me, a Tunisian man stares pensively into a window that looks into an identical window that looks into an identical car a second ahead of where we are. He is carrying a door, hugged against his body and giving him a look of borrowed stability. The mirror gets up and walks past me as I chance to turn my head: sudden conjunction in the glass of the buttons of the woman's *manteau* (like a row of eyes, they look out at me) and a patch of browngreenpink stripes of my poncho, a streak of dull gold hair—before it moves off and out into the night, where so many reflections are glimmering or are about to come into their own.

METRO MARQUIS DE SADE

YOU MAY FIND YOURSELF NEEDING THE FOLLOWING USEFUL ALIBI:

❋ I'm sorry I'm late, darling, but I was impaled at the Métro de Sade, and it took three adorable brutes to free me, and then two happening-by mauvais-garçons-manqués to deliver me from them.

❋ *Désolée d'être en retard, chéri, mais j'étais empalée au métro de Sade, et il a fallu trois belles brutes pour me libérer, puis deux mauvais-garçons-manqués qui passaient pour me délivrer d'eux.*

For more about the Métro Marquis de Sade please see Métro Récamier on the next page.

METRO RECAMIER

Récamier is the one métro station where people go out of their way to rendezvous (besides the Hôtel Taupique, catering to two extremes of the social spectrum, the rich with their *clochard* counterparts snoozing at their expense) and where the *clochards* make reservations weeks in advance for one night of plush, rakish slumbers, with or without *chocolat*.

Listening in the métro corridor to harp, accordion, and guitar playing: then some delicate tapping sounds, and four young blind ones come stepping down the stairs. I often forget that I am myself visible, I live so much through my eyes.

Métro Récamier, the most posh and popular station of all, was created as a monument to a métro car that *did* exist in the bellest époque the underground has ever known, a car that was furnished with reclining couches and sprawling, recumbent passengers.

The big draw in Métro Récamier is the furniture: no mere grafitti'd benches with yogurt and Greek islands advertised on the walls, but the same couches that used to travel, here bolted down. This extravagance is supported by contributions from several cultural societies in Paris dedicated to preserving a gracious past in the most unlikely places. If you have trouble finding a place to park your *arse poetica* (see Stores and Shopping) you can take it to the faraway Square Chaise Récamier off rue de la Chaise (your pants will know right where they are). So pleasantly at ease, not many at Métro Récamier actually board the métro cars coming through, so sometimes the train whooshes right past and on to the next stop. Sooner or later one will pause to open its doors, but don't use this station if your destination is demanding you show up on time. On the same line, the nearby Métro Marquis de Sade has spikes on the seats, where only the masochists tend to dally. This is the way to go if time is of consequence.

VILLE DE PARIS

LOST AND FOUND/PERDU ET TROUVE
Français au verso

Please fill out the following form with a description of the lost article(s).

Description: A greyhound can't get lost, that's what my vet tells me. He thinks I've ditched him. His name is Baraka—the dog's name, that is, not the vet's. The vet, whose name is Simon, thinks he's more of a psychiatrist than a dog doctor. But why I would get rid of such a blessed creature— Baraka means blessed, you know; and with his soulful eyes, you'd almost believe you were talking to a saint. At least, that's how I feel. I lost him in the métro. Oh, I see, I write that down below. To comply with RATP regulations, I bought a lovely *Lady and the Unicorn* tapestry bag for him to stick his head, tail, and much of his body out of—while he held court in the métro car—what with his eyes which I've described, and his gentle **Approximate Location of Lost Object:**   manner of shaking hands even with drunks. One old lady, who always rides at the same time, knitted him a cap to go with his bag. He was wearing it (earth-tone to match his own **Approximate Time and Date Object Lost:**   hair) when he got lost. Down in the métro. We were off to Asnières to visit a relative who passed away. His, not mine, Asnières being a pet cemetery as everyone knows. But, I just can't quite remember when I noticed he was gone. Greyhounds have a way of blending in, of just being there and then not being there. Yes, yes, I know he's my dog and I'm supposed to keep him on a leash but you can't tie up a saint with a strip of leather, can you?

METRO MIRO

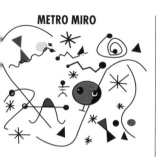

This station is decorated with Miró's paintings. Many visitors to Paris find themselves attempting to follow these paintings on the assumption that they are maps of the subway routes. They end up having ferociously right-angle escapades and curvaceously alluring detours in the métro and just afterward. (See also Métro Mondrian.)

METRO MEMOIRE

Métro Mémoire might make a fitful stopover at the Hôtel Hélas, and when it's on the move, it sends shivers down the line.

In more ways than one, the Métro Mémoire goes deeper than the underground. When you have the time, you can take it to the Café Passé Composé and have, with your Viennoiserie and reflections (see also Métro Miroir), a café imparfait. If you don't feel like conjugating your life in these past tenses or recalling your many *faux pas,* there's always Café Sans Souci, without a care, but you'll have to transfer several times to reach it.

METRO MIROIR

Passengers tend to become reflective when pausing in this station of mirrors and pools. Conceptualist artist Ricky Souslesvignes created the echo chambers to complete the version of the myth in which Narcissus rebuffed Echo's love for him and was thereupon punished with facing himself for eternity.

Alluding to the flames of persecution during the Spanish Inquisition and owned by German-Belgian entrepreneur Otto Dafé, Auto da Fée isn't hot at all, but bases its cars (flamboyant taxis and joyrides for tourists) on *le monde féerique,* fairyland, and they are among the most picturesque sights in motion as you traverse the city. Thanks to artists in need of a grant from the Ministry of Culture, no single set of headlights resembles another, and it's even rare for the same pair to match. In the early morning hours, with little traffic about, one of these vehicles appears from a distance like an enormous firefly scurrying down la rue de Rivoli, or a Chinese lantern swinging over le Pont des Invalides. But there's nothing cute or infantile about this company—don't start signing up the kiddies for the next Easter vacation on Air France, or working yourself up into your own Ludwig of Bavaria delusions. These taxis resemble more closely in demeanor and elegance the coaches of the *demimondaine* (courtesan) out for a drive in the Bois de Boulogne, and the cost is commensurate with this pretentious charade. They are popular with drug dealers, foreign potentates, high-class call girls, publishers, the occasional minister or *artiste.* The rest of us drink deeply of their extravagance, for no matter how luxurious and fantastic the interiors, it's the vision through the fog, the rain, the lonely night that keeps these cars and our thoughts afloat.

TAXIS
AUTO DA FEE

"So there it was. I left the hermetic paradise [of Saint-Laurent's home] and went out into a drizzling Paris whose taxi drivers seemed all to have gone on vacation. . . . I trudged, wincing at the toothache in my calf, over the greasy pebbles to that Métro whose turnstiles could never admit a Saint-Laurent creation. . . ."

—Anthony Burgess

The Autos da Fée bring their joy to the streets thanks to the Minister of Culture, early Mitterand reign, who engaged artists in Paris from around the world to fashion the headlights and paint, sculpt, rig the *voitures,* so many of their creations are based on distant empires' legends and tales or imaginations fed by them. The exorbitant profits from these colorful rides fund other projects that allow artists to extend their visas and pay for their miserable *chambres de bonne,* maid rooms with sloping ceilings and up eight flights of stairs, the final flight usually too narrow for most maids.

TAXIS
ÇA VA CHAUFFER!

APROPOS PROTEST:
☞ Am I paying for this other passenger as well? This menagerie of brioches, millefeuilles, and fur hats?
☜ *Est-ce que je paie aussi pour cet autre passager? Cette ménagerie de brioches, millefeuilles, et ces chapeaux en fourrure?*

A limo service that originally misspelled its name Les Chauffers de Montmartre, *chauffer* meaning to heat up. Now when their cars go by people yell out "Ça va chauffer!," the French equivalent of our dire prediction "the fur's going to fly," and that is how the company has come to be known. *Boulangeries* and *pâtisseries* throughout Paris have simply refused to comprehend that these taxis are no toastier than most, and use them to deliver *baguettes, pains au chocolat, ficelles,* and *pains passion* as if hot out of the oven when the stuff is really a half-day old.

It must be added, though, that in deference to the many linguistic complexities entangling their

cars and this page, the company does show pref-
erence in hiring wild, hairy Georgians with
astrakhan caps as their drivers, and insists the poor
fellows keep on wearing them through the sweltering summer months, just to humor whichever
British and American tourists know the idiomatic
analogue of *ça va chauffer.* One of the more enter-
prising such Georgians, with gangster connec-
tions back home, got his revenge by starting a
business whose *real* name is The Fur's Going to
Fly: a helicopter service that delivers fur coats to
the wealthy women of Paris, London, Vienna,
Berlin by dropping the parcels onto their balconies. The pilots, many of them former athletes,
take pride in being good shots, and sometimes
have to fight off the Animal Rights Patrol, which
has in turn taken to the air. Exceedingly affluent
himself by now, our Georgian tycoon has his own
helicopter—and sweltering chauffeur—lined with
fox, mink, and raccoon.

Lesson in sheep:

Revenons à nos moutons!:
Let's return to the sub-
ject. Some Parisians don't
have sheepskin covers for
car seats, but drive around
with live sheep in their
laps. Thus "Revenons à
nos moutons!" is also the
cry of the man roaming
the levels of the parking
structure in search of his
bleating Peugeot.

Orféo is the one bus that does not punish or
expel musicians; in fact, auditions are de
rigueur here. For the omnibusker of no small
promise, this can be the start of something big.
Talents launched on the Orféo are booted into the
arena to play for the crowds, *critiques,* and applause
(see Nightlife and Entertainment, Les Arènes de

BUSES
ORFEO

BUSES
EURYDICE

THE CATACOMBS

LA COUPOLE

BUSES
TZIGANE

"To want a world is fire—
to obtain it, smoke."
—Tzigane saying

Tobermory).You are expected to pay for these *divertissements,* whatever you can cough up, and count yourself lucky to do so. Years later, you can say, "Why, I first heard that guy on his sax (or cello, zemba, flute) between the Gare du Nord and Parc Chauve-Souris with my fiancée on my knees." Sometimes when musicians are jamming you forget where you were going and start improvising on your life. Well, isn't that why you travel, to recall such sensations?

The Eurydice Express (once connected to Orféo) disappears underground when it hits Denfert-Rochereau. Passengers are taking their chances with this one: not many can resist the backward glance. It's probably safer just to pay your respects to Rabelais in the Catacombs (entrance nearby) and emerge a half hour later with silt in your shoes, mud on your knees, and a mild case of claustrophobia, all of which you can shake off shortly in the spacious splendor of La Coupole, on boulevard Montparnasse.

Tzigane is especially accommodating to those with no particular destination and with large bundles, lives rattling in assorted appliances, bangles, blackened pots and pans. Smoking is not only allowed, it's encouraged if your cigarettes

are Gitanes—and women, please cover your
ankles, so lascivious they should not be seen.

Yes, this sounds like a restaurant on rue Bouffe-
tard, but it's really a bus line that follows strict
geometrical patterns and serves tiropitas,
spanakopitas, and little sandwiches and pastries
cut in squares, rhomboids, triangles, parallelo-
grams. (Some of the Beaux-Arts architecture students work in the Archimède kitchen, getting
practice for a lifetime of making *maquettes*—see
Hôtels, Hôtel Mostar.) With its penchant for
grids, this bus service spends much time outside
Paris or driving through courtyards and parks
when no one's looking.

BUSES
AUX DELICES
D'ARCHIMEDE

Alternate route to
Péripherique is the
Pathétique

Marelle (Hopscotch, named for the Cortázar
novel set in Paris and Buenos Aires) goes to
and from the Pont des Arts, connects with the 62
bus sometimes, and deposits the rare suggestible
customer near the axolotls in the Jardin des
Plantes (see Nightlife and Entertainment, Le
Trottoir de Buenos Aires). The Marelle has a sim-
patico rapport with the Minotaure line, which
goes through labyrinths, metaphysical or otherwise. If this leaves you confounded, a few sessions
with a specialist from Philosophe a l'Heure
should somewhat straighten you out.

BUSES
MARELLE

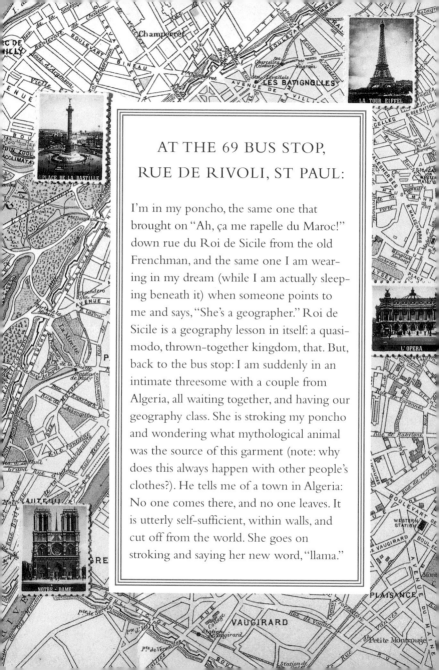

AT THE 69 BUS STOP, RUE DE RIVOLI, ST PAUL:

I'm in my poncho, the same one that brought on "Ah, ça me rapelle du Maroc!" down rue du Roi de Sicile from the old Frenchman, and the same one I am wearing in my dream (while I am actually sleeping beneath it) when someone points to me and says, "She's a geographer." Roi de Sicile is a geography lesson in itself: a quasi-modo, thrown-together kingdom, that. But, back to the bus stop: I am suddenly in an intimate threesome with a couple from Algeria, all waiting together, and having our geography class. She is stroking my poncho and wondering what mythological animal was the source of this garment (note: why does this always happen with other people's clothes?). He tells me of a town in Algeria: No one comes there, and no one leaves. It is utterly self-sufficient, within walls, and cut off from the world. She goes on stroking and saying her new word, "llama."

A FAREWELL TO THE READER

Our revels are not now ending, and your travels are just beginning. We leave you in the transportation zone that you might be transported in mind or body wherever you wish to go. Make your arrangements, take your derangements, mail us a postcard from La Poste du Pont Traversé, on the bridge between desire and fulfillment. Welcome, then, to your very own footsteps, walking you to Café Destinée, to meet another Out of Hander at the Museum of Lips and Books or take flight in a hushed hotel. Paris is yours for the asking, and we hope you've found new questions, not answers, as you set off to uncover both the bright side and the night side of *your* unparalleled tracks. Windows want your eyes, faces await your reflections, the life of a city calls for yours to enter.

The map on this page illustrates Paris after the great monuments en mouvement, *monuments on the move, planned along with other festivities for the publication of* Paris Out of Hand.

P. 53: Guillaume Apollinaire, from *Alcools,* translated by Anne Hyde Greet. © 1965 by The Regents of the University of California. Berkeley: University of California Press, 1965.

P. 82: Guillaume Apollinaire, from "La jolie rousse" ("The Pretty Redhead"), from *Calligrammes,* © 1925 by Editions Gallimard. "The Pretty Redhead" translated by James Wright, from *Collected Poems,* by James Wright. Hanover, N. H.: Wesleyan University Press, 1971.

P. 75: Louis Aragon, from "Tapestry of the Great Fear," translated by Malcolm Cowley, from *Le Crève-cœur.* France: Librairie Gallimard, 1941.

Pp. 11, 87, 132, 146: Louis Aragon, from *Paris Peasant,* translated by Simon Watson Taylor. Translation © 1971 by Jonathan Cape Ltd. London: Picador Classics, 1987.

P. 60: Honoré de Balzac, "Colonel Chabert," from *The Short Stories of Balzac.* New York: Dial Press, 1948.

P. 84: Charles Baudelaire, "The Eyes of the Poor." *The Parisian Prowler: Le Spleen de Paris. Petits Poèmes en prose.* Translated by Edward K. Kaplan. © 1989 by Edward K. Kaplan. Athens, Georgia: The University of Georgia Press, 1989.

P. 51: Nina Berberova, from "The Tattered Cloak," from *The Tattered Cloak and Other Novels,* translated from the Russian by Marian Schwartz. © 1990, 1991, by Marian Schwartz. New York: Alfred A. Knopf, Inc., 1991.

P. 28: André Breton, from "A Man and Woman Absolutely White," from *Clair de Terre,* © 1966 by Editions Gallimard. Reprinted by Permission of Georges Borchardt for Editions Gallimard. Translated by David Antin, translation reprinted by permission of David Antin.

Pp. 104, 118: André Breton, from "Vigilance," from *Clair de Terre,* preceded by *Mont de Piété,* followed by *Le Revolver à cheveux blancs* and *L'Air de l'eau* (1966). "Monde" ("World") taken from *Poèmes* (1949). © 1949, 1966 by Editions Gallimard. Translation © 1966 by Michael Benedikt (from Breton's *Poèmes*). Translation © 1949 by Michael Benedikt. Reprinted by permission of Georges Borchardt, Inc.

P. 124: André Breton, from *Nadja,* translated by Richard Howard. © 1960 by Grove Press, Inc. New York: Grove Press, Inc., 1960.

Pp. 67, 153: Anthony Burgess, *Homage to Qwert Yuiop.* © 1986 Anthony Burgess. London: Hutchinson, 1986.

P. 104: Blaise Cendrars, from *To the End of the World,* translated from the French by Alan Brown. Translation © 1966 by Alan Brown. New York: Grove Press, Inc. Originally published as *Emmène-moi au Bout du Monde* by Editions Denoël, Paris. © 1956 by Editions Denoël, Paris.

P. 141: Colette, from "My Corset Maker," from *The Collected Stories of Colette,* edited by Robert Phelps and translated by Matthew Ward. Translation © 1983 by Farrar, Straus & Giroux, Inc. Translation © 1984 by Martin Secker and Warburg Ltd. London: Martin Secker and Warburg Ltd., 1958. Reprinted by permission of Farrar, Straus & Giroux.

P. 129: Julio Cortázar, excerpt from *Paris: Essence of an Image,* essay accompanying photographs by Alecio de Andrade. Translated from the Spanish by Gregory Rabassa. © 1981 by Julio Cortázar. Geneva: RotoVision S.A., 1981.

P. 62: *Sonia Delaunay: Rhythms and Colors,* Boston: Little, Brown and Company, 1971. Originally published as *Sonia Delaunay: Rythymes et Couleurs,* Jacques Dumase, editor. Paris: Hermann, 1971. Reprinted by permission of Little, Brown and Company.

P. 82: Lawrence Durrell, from *Balthazar.* © 1958 by Lawrence Durrell. London: Faber and Faber, 1962.

Pp. 28, 94: Richard Ellman, from *Oscar Wilde.* © 1988 by Richard Ellman. New York: Alfred A. Knopf, 1988.

P. 101: Richard Ellman, from *James Joyce.* © 1959, 1982 by Richard Ellman. Rev. ed. New York: Oxford University Press, 1982.

Pp. 99, 156: Edmond de Goncourt, from *Pages from the Goncourt Journal,* edited, translated, and introduced by Robert Baldick. Translation © 1962 by Robert Baldick. London: Oxford University Press, 1962.

P. 135: Max Jacob, from "Ballad of the Night Visitor," translated by William Kulik, from *The American Poetry Review,* March/April 1994, and Kulik's work in progress, *The Selected Poems of Max Jacob.* Printed with permission of William Kulik.

P. 20: Gilbert Lascault, from *Un Monde Miné.* Paris: Christian Bourgois Editeur, 1975.

P. 117: Osip Mandelstam, from "The French," in *Journey to Armenia,* from *The Noise of Time: The Prose of Osip Mandelstam,* translated by Clarence Brown. © 1965 by Princeton University Press. San Francisco: North Point Press, 1986.

Pp. 60, 63: George D. Painter, *Proust: The later years.* © 1965 by George Painter. Boston: Little, Brown and Company, 1965.

P. 125: Jean-Jacques Passera, from "Paris" in *Exquisite Corpse.* © 1985, 1995 by Jean-Jacques Passera. Printed with permission of Jean-Jacques Passera.

Pp. 112, 124: Frederick Prokosch, from *Voices: A Memoir.* © 1983 by Frederick Prokosch. New York: Farrar, Straus & Giroux, Inc., 1983.

P. 143: Raymond Queneau, from *Excercises in Style,* translated by Barbara Wright. © 1947 by Editions Gallimard. © 1958, 1981 by Barbara Wright. © 1958 by Gaberbocchus Press. New York: New Directions Publishing Corporation, 1981.

Pp. 103, 106: Raymond Queneau, from *Zazie in the Métro,* translated by Barbara Wright. Translation © 1960, 1982 by Barbara Wright. London: John Calder Publishers, Ltd., 1982.

Pp. 40, 107, 116: Rainer Maria Rilke, from *The Notebook of Malte Laurids Brigge,* translated by John Linton. Translation © 1930 by The Hogarth Press. London: The Hogarth Press, 1972.

P. 80: Jacques Roubaud, *Roubaud's Law of Butter Croissants,* from *The Great Fire of London: A story with interpolations and bifurcations,* translated by Dominic Di Bernardi. Originally published by Editions de Seuil, © 1989 by Editions du Seuil. Translation © 1991 by Dominic Di Bernardi. Reprinted with permission of Dalkey Archive Press, Normal, Illinois.

P. 134: Claude Royet-Journoud, from "The Crowded Circle," originally published as "Le Cercle nombreux," in *Le Renversement,* © 1972 by Editions Gallimard. Translated by Keith Waldrop, from *Reversal.* Hellcoal First Edition Series, 1973.

P. 120: Maya Sonenberg, from "Nature Morte," in *Cartographies.* © 1989 by Maya Sonenberg. Hopewell, N. J.: Ecco Press, 1990. Reprinted by permission of The Ecco Press.

P. 19, 95: Paul Valery, from "The Bath," translated by Louise Varèse, and from "Song of the Master-Idea," from *Selected Writings of Paul Valéry.* © 1950 by New Directions. New York: New Directions Publishing Corp., 1950. Reprinted by permission of New Directions Publishing Corp.